VIRTUE AND MORALITY

About the Author

Xavier Pfokrehe Mao is a specialist in moral, social and political philosophy with special reference to Northeast. He has obtained his M.Phil. Degree from Delhi University on a National Junior Research Fellowship (JRF) and M.Lett. from University of Sydney, Australia on an Australian International Development Scholarship (AUSAIDS). He did his Ph.D. from North Eastern Hill University, Shillong. He has been teaching in NEHU since 1988 with regular contribution to the media on significant public debates and issues.

His numerous papers mainly on North East India and contemporary life, politics and society have been published. He has also contributed papers in more than a dozen edited books.

To

My Son

Maphrio

Who lightens up my World

VIRTUE AND MORALITY

Dr. Xavier Pfokrehe Mao
Department of Philosophy
North Eastern Hill University
Shillong

CONCEPT PUBLISHING COMPANY PVT. LTD.
NEW DELHI-110059

ISBN-13: 978-81-8069-763-0

First Published 2011

Published and Printed by

Concept
Since 1974

Concept Publishing Company Pvt. Ltd.
Regd. Office:
A/15-16, Commercial Block, Mohan Garden
New Delhi-110059 (India)
Phones : 25351460, 25351794, *Fax* : 091-11-25357109
Email : publishing@conceptpub.com
Website: www.conceptpub.com

Editorial Office:
H-13, Bali Nagar, New Delhi-110 015, India.

Cataloging in Publication Data--*Courtesy:* D.K. Agencies (P) Ltd. <docinfo@dkagencies.com>

Mao, Xavier Pfokrehe.
Virtue and morality / Xavier Pfokrehe Mao.
p. cm.
Includes bibliographical references (p.) and index.
ISBN 9788180697630

1. Ethics. 2. Virtues. 3. Life--Moral and ethical aspects. I. Title.

DDC 170 22

Preface

The book is written in pursuit of contemporary dilemmas within Moral Philosophy and beyond. Especially what has now come to be known as moral quandaries in matters of determining the right and the good become a subject of serious contemplation in this book. It pertains to a topic of great interest to students of philosophy who are doing a course of research in Western moral philosophy. Further, it will be also interesting to teachers and non-philosophy readers who have keen interest in matters of morality, life and philosophy. With this end in view, I thought to make it available to the general community of students, teachers and other readers who are interested in the present day moral philosophy. In fact, this topic is of general interest because of the sudden revival of Virtue Ethics as against what I called the Act Morality. But in real life situation, a person needs both virtues and standards of moral judgements. This book perhaps, provides a guide to those who are interested in bringing considerations of the quality of character and standards of right action for their personal and social moral behaviour.

December 12, 2009 **Xavier Pfokrehe Mao**

Professor **M. M. Agrawal**
B.A., Ph.D. (London)
Professor of Culture and Philosophy

A-273, Block B
Ramprastha Colony Ghaziabad
Uttar Pradesh 201011
Mobile: 9818304353

Foreword

In this work Dr. Mao undertakes a rather difficult task of assessing the relative merit of two completely different approaches to moral philosophizing. In one, which he calls 'ACT MORALITY', which has held the primary position in modern ethical studies, philosophers have conducted a search for a single supreme moral principle from which the diverse moral rules could be derived and unified under one banner. Here the assumption is that individual acts rather than persons performing those acts, are primary objects of moral evaluation. And it is the primary concern of the moral philosopher to produce a criterion or standard of correct moral judgement applicable in all the diverse moral situations in which a person finds himself in actual real life.

As opposed to this, the other approach, which he calls 'Virtue Ethics', holds persons, their character, virtues and vices as the primary focus of Ethical studies. Ever since the publication of After Virtue by Alasdair McIntyre, this other approach has had a flourishing reception in Moral Philosophy.

Dr. Mao conducts the debate between these two competing approaches in admirably lively fashion. After a detailed discussion of their respective positions, he rightly concludes that "the contingencies of historical, social and personal nature create at time morally relevant considerations" which cannot be morally evaluated from the timeless abstract perspective of Act Morality. On the other hand, the greatest flow with Virtue Ethics lies in the fact that it fails to develop either the 'ratio' or the 'ordinatio' of virtues, which leaves the individual "choice" in real situation of conflict, in real quandary, and with an arbitrariness and indecisiveness, generally unacceptable in ethical behaviour.

All in all the discussion is insightful and is bound to leave an urge for further reading and enquiry in any intelligent reader of Moral Philosophy.

September 6, 2010

M. M. Agrawal

CONTENTS

Acknowledgements

This book is based on my many years of engagement with Moral Philosophy at Universities of Delhi and Sydney and also at North Eastern Hill University, Shillong. In this endeavour I am deeply grateful to Professors Murari Mohan Agrawal, Netrananda Malla, John Grumley, George Marcus, Margaret Chatterjee and V. P. Gaur for having very useful critical discussion with me. All these teachers, colleagues and friends benefited me by their enlightened interventions in my thought process. I am also grateful to my colleagues and students in the Department. of Philosophy at NEHU, Shillong. Especially, I am appreciative of Dr. Prasenjit Biswas for helping me in preparation of the index and for engaging in fruitful interactions.

Lastly, I owe a profound gratitude to my wife Kusha for her encouragement and support that she always gave to me.

1

INTRODUCTION
MORAL CONFUSION TODAY

Modern moral theories have failed adding to confusion in moral philosophy. From the beginning of Enlightenment, modern moral theories have been following a kind of enterprise which Alasdair MacIntyre has called "The Enlightenment Project of Justifying Morality".[1] This presupposes a certain view of morality as we practice it. In their view, moral property and quality are to be assigned to individual choices. These choices are made in the light of a supreme moral principle from which particular rules of morality can be seen to follow. Thus, the logic of moral choice is almost syllogistic. The individual is supposed to use moral principles and a statement about the situation he is in, as major premise, from which the conclusion about what action he is to choose to perform follows. Modern moral philosophers then, made it a project for themselves to justify that their fundamental principles are values of their moral system and the only correct principles are values.

These theories, from the point of view of the standards they prescribe fall into three groups :

1. Utilitarianism
2. Intuitionism
3. Rationalism

Following a broader sort of division, the theories under these headings fall all under what is known as naturalistic and non-naturalistic theories.

According to the above mentioned modern moral theories, the relevant question is what is the factor in action or choice which determines the rightness or wrongness of an action? According to Utilitarianism, it is the consequence of an action which is the determining factor. According to intuitionism, it is the moral intuition. For Kantianism, it is the motive which decides the rightness or wrongness of an act. All the three types are in the same boat because each excludes the other. What is common to all these theories is that in judging the rightness or wrongness of an action, they claim, several factors have to be taken into account.

These insights apply to all modern moral theories as Pincoffs points out that modern moral theories are "reductive". What he means by this is that the modern moral theories take one or other important aspect of moral practice and treat it as a paradigm for judging the whole area in which we are said to act morally. In other words, they are not only reductive but also exclusivist. They tend to ignore factors other than their own chosen ones in judging the rightness or wrongness of actions. As all these types of theories have actually failed, thereby have given rise to the claims of Emotivism in this century. But Emotivism has also failed completely In fact, as MacIntyre has pointed out, Emotivism is not a theory of morality at all, but a theory of the 'use' of moral words, rather I should say that is a theory of moral words.

In my book, in the following chapters, I shall examine a representative version of each of these theories in some detail. But for the time being I only wish to point out that the failure of these theories has created a kind of uncertainty and confusion in moral philosophy which in turn has made contemporary philosophers to rethink about the whole business of moral philosophizing. Consequently, the philosophy which has come to be termed as Virtue Ethics has emerged. It is from the time of publication of *After Virtue* of MacIntyre that Virtue Ethics has acquired prominence in the field of ethics or moral philosophy.

In this context, the reason for the failure of pre-virtue Ethics theories are most important, because they claim to justify the turn in moral philosophizing towards Virtue Ethics. Broadly, a moral theory may fail for two different sorts of reason. It may fail for lack of internal coherence and persuasiveness in its argument for its claim. On the other hand, it may be that somehow its whole approach or fundamental way is misguided. It is for the latter sort of reasons that virtue ethics claims to reject the modern moral theories and puts its own approach in its place. In examining these theories, therefore, I will be particularly concerned with the claim of Virtue Ethics in respect of why the modern theories have actually failed. And further, I will be concerned with evaluation of the claim that the failure of these theories justify a whole sole rejection of their whole approach to ethics. In this part of my book, I shall take MacIntyre's views as a representative of Virtue Ethics. This is not to say that other works will not be referred to. In contemporary literature on the subject, there is a lively debate which cannot be ignored in arriving at one's preference of the right approach to Morality or Ethics. In other words, I will attempt to arrive at judgment for or against the rival approaches to see if one is to be rejected completely or it needs some kind of modification.

But before I proceed to undertake this examination, I would like to spell out the salient features of the two approaches, which I have named as *Rule Morality* and *Character Ethics* respectively.

In Rule Morality, moral philosophers have taken for granted that morality primarily concerns with evaluation of *acts* or *human conduct*. Acts or conduct are considered as the main moral phenomena and the assessment of their rightness or wrongness is the primary moral task. In day-to-day life, we make moral judgments upon actual or possible pieces of behaviour of others or our own selves on the basis of certain principles which we normally take for granted. In fact, these principles are presupposed in all cases of a judgment and they are handed down to us from generation to generation. In ordinary moral life, the moral agent is often not even aware of the presupposition of moral judgment. This is where moral philosopher comes in. The task of a moral philosopher is first to bring the presuppositions like the principles, values, beliefs, etc. of our moral judgments into the open and then to inquire into the justification of holding those presuppositions and basing our conduct upon them. In particular, the moral philosopher inquires if the principles or beliefs in question have *rational* justification, or they are simply customary. Since morality is concerned not only with how people actually behave but with how they *ought* to behave. It should be possible to justify its recommendations. In Rule Morality, the moral philosopher imagines that the rules of conduct which are considered right form into a system which is internally consistent. They further believe that the rules of conduct can be justified by reference to a single and supreme principle or morality, or a set of principles which are consistent with each other. The task of a moral philosopher, then is to formulate the supreme principle of morality in terms of which moral justification is made. In history of moral philosophy, different standards of morality have been suggested. But all of them seem to have a common vision of the task of moral philosophy. Fundamentally, they believe that whatever principles are presupposed in moral life, can explain the moral phenomena exhaustively. The Rules moralists try to answer the following questions: What determines the rightness or wrongness of acts or conduct? In their view, whatever that makes actions right or wrong can ultimately solve all moral problems. In Rules Morality, therefore, the assessment of other moral phenomena such as the moral agents and their character traits, their capacities, their motives are secondary. But in day-to-day life we often judge people and their character though for the act of moralist, such judgments are derivative from judgments about their acts, i.e., our acts are taken as objective entities to which the stipulated moral standards apply directly. But the moral agency and its traits and attributes are subjective phenomena which accrues only through the objective acts. Some moral philosophers even hold that motives and other qualities of character, for example, are not at all relevant to assessment of moral acts. Some moral philosophers even hold that motives and other qualities of character, for example, are not at all relevant to assessment of moral acts.

It is at this point that the sharp contrast between act or Rule Morality and character morality or virtue ethics appears. For the virtue ethics philosophers, the primary object of moral assessment is the moral agent himself. Since the moral agency is constituted by the quality of character and motive etc. Moral judgments about a person are primarily in terms of qualities and motives which signify certain virtues. The assessment of acts, then, are secondary to virtue. But the standards for judging individual acts are obtained from the actual examples of kinds of things a virtuous person will naturally do in the relevant situation. According to this view, therefore, the primary concern of a moral philosopher should be with virtues. He should tell us which qualities of character are to be counted as virtues and why. The philosophical discussion of the identity and unity of virtues is at the centre of virtue-ethics. In advocating things, virtue ethics hopes to replace act morality view in moral philosophy.

The current debate in virtue ethics began with the appearance of the article *Modern Moral Philosophy* by G.E.M. Anscombe where she called for a reconsideration of the Aristotelian ethics centering round the notion of goodness, character and virtue.[2] She claimed this to be the real concern of ethics. Later, this was followed up by the works of Phillipa Foot and Bernard Williams among others. But it is MacIntyre's *After Virtue* (1981) which put virtue ethics on the pedestal of moral philosopher. By now, there is a considerable variety of literature on the subject. However, there are certain claims in virtue ethics which seem to be common to all the variety of views on the subject. Later in my book I will discuss these claims in great detail. For now, however, I wish to list the most essential features of virtue ethics as follows :

1. The most important claims of virtue ethics concern with determination of rightness of an action. It claims that an action is right if and only if it is of the type which a virtuous agent would naturally do in a given situation. In this claim, what is asserted is that any justification of an action must refer to the *character* of an agent. What *makes* an action right is that it flows from the character of a virtuous person. The virtuous person typically performs that action in that sort of situation. Thus, for example, it would be right to save someone's life which is good to him because this is mostly that a benevolent person would do. A benevolent person acts in that manner because benevolence is a virtue which aims at the good of others. So a benevolent person would be naturally disposed to act to help others.[3]
2. The second central claim in virtue ethics concerns itself with the priority of goodness over rightness. What this means is that the notion of goodness is primary and rightness can be defined only in relation to goodness. We cannot determine the rightness of an action unless and until we have explained what is valuable or good. For virtue ethics, this means that the moral philosopher has to give an account of *human* good in terms of admirable and intrinsically good human traits. Only by reference to such intrinsically good human character traits, can we determine what is the right thing to do in a given situation.
3. The third class is about plurality of virtues. What

this means is that the account of human good which justifies an action as right includes a number of virtues which are essential for a humanly flourishing life and for being a virtuous agent. These qualities or virtues signify a plurality of values which are not reducible to or derivable from some supreme value. This is so because virtues are to be taken as *intrinsically* valuable rather than merely instrumental. In other words, virtues are valuable for their own sake and not for the sake of realizing something which is valuable, as in the well-known example in which Aristotle maintains the friendship is 'Choice-worthy in itself' and not valuable for the advantage which it may bring to one.

4. The real essential feature of virtue ethics is that virtues are held to be objectively good. The objectivity in question here is to be contrasted with the subjectivity of desire. Virtues are objectively good for their connection with essential human characteristic. For example, theoretical and practical rationality, or for example, their connection with character traits which are in themselves admirable. Thus courage will be held as objectively valuable independently of whether or not the courageous person himself desires to be courageous.
5. Some values are regarded, for example, friendship, integrity and justice, as agent-neutral. What it means is that my friendship will have special relevance for my moral action which other person's friendship may not have. Finally, a connected point is that rightness of an action cannot be determined in terms of attempt to realize the maximum human good. Thus, for example, virtue ethics does not require us to *maximize* my friendship. What it

> requires is simply that I should have good friendship (where good is understood by the attitudes which govern such relationships).

In the forthcoming chapter my main aim will be to contrast Act Morality with Virtue Ethics on the essential points as sketched above. This will, I hope, put us in a position to adjudicate between the relative merits of the two views. But before we embark on this, in order to make room for virtue ethics, we have to see if the Act Morality is really in a hopeless situation. The best way of ascertaining this is to consider representative form of Act Morality views and to examine them in respect of their internal and external deficiencies. This, I propose to do in the next three chapters.

REFERENCES

1. A. MacIntyre. *After Virtue,* Duckworth, 1985, p.36.
2. *Philosophy,* 33, 1958.
3. *Cf.* Phillipa Foot. *Euthanasia,* pp. 44-45.

2

UTILITARIANISM

In modern moral philosophy various theories attempt at producing a *standard* of rightness of action which could be applied generally to judging human action. They then attempt to justify their respective standards claiming that their standard or standards are the only correct ones. In order to understand Act Morality or Rule Morality, therefore, it is better to consider some representative standards and see how they are arrived at. We can then raise the question about the suitability of doing this kind of moral philosophy.

Traditionally, three sorts of standards have been invoked. These are to be found in Utilitarianism, Intuitionism and Kantianism. In the present chapter, I will consider Utilitarianism.

In Utilitarianism we find an attractive and popular standard of moral rightness of action. Put simply, it holds that an action is right if it is useful for promoting happiness. Generally and most succinctly said by J.S. Mill, it is held that happiness is the sum total of pleasures. Pleasure is good in itself. What is called hedonistic utilitarianism holds that pleasure alone is good in itself, i.e. to be desired for its own sake. Other things like love, knowledge, truth and beauty are also good but they are good only in so far as they are productive of pleasure, or in so far as they are pleasurable in themselves. There is, however, another form of utilitarianism called Ideal utilitarianism. In this form, other things like love, knowledge, etc. are also considered as ends in themselves. They are also good as pleasure. However, both forms have this in common that they believe that the rightness of an act is its utility, its usefulness in producing results which are seen as good as in themselves. For my purpose, it is the consideration of this common principle that is important.

1. Can utility be a criterion or the sole criterion of rightness of action?
2. Can the consideration of the rightness of action be the sole purpose of moral evaluation?
3. Can moral philosophy of this kind capture the vast complexity of actual moral life?

These are the most important questions which I wish to answer in my thesis. It is in the light of these answers that we will be able to judge the relative merits of the Act Morality *versus* Virtue Ethics.

There are several stock arguments against utilitarianism. Most of them relate to the internal incoherence in the utilitarian thesis. One very important criticism of this kind claims that their fundamental notion of happiness itself is not a unitary notion. That is, happiness is not the name of a single state of mind which is promoted by the production of things which are good, which in case of hedonistic utilitarianism as we saw above is itself only pleasure. It is pointed out that pleasures themselves are different qualitatively depending upon the nature of the activities which produce them. Similarly, happiness differs in kind and not only in degree. The happiness of the contemplative way of life such as that of Socrates cannot be compared with the happiness say for example, of a successful cricketer. Mill is supposed to have realized this problem in criticizing in Bentham's handling of the concept of happiness. It is reflected in the famous dictum "It is better to be Socrates dissatisfied than a pig satisfied". Later, however, Sidgwick realized the complete disunity of our moral belief. He realized that our moral beliefs are heterogeneous and the ends which we pursue as good do not derive their goodness from their pleasure producing qualities if they have such a quality at all. Sidgwick claims that at the bottom of our moral thinking there are beliefs about human goods which have no further justification. They are, what Sidgwick terms our fundamental moral *intuitions*. If this is true as it seems to me, then it has further implications for the principle of utility to be regarded as the sole criterion of moral rightness. It is a fact that the principle of utility maintains that actions are right if they are useful in promoting happiness. But now the crucial question arises: Whose happiness? The utilitarians tell us to maximize happiness and for maximum number of people as well. But should it be the dissatisfied Socratic kind of happiness or the "pig type" of happiness? It may be that it is better to have a few Socratic type of happy people in a society than to have a large number of people who are satisfied with a lower form of happiness. The issue is difficult to resolve. There seems to be no easy answer both to the question of the quality of happiness and the number of people whose happiness is to be ensured. The truth is that happiness is very specific to individual forms of life lived by individuals. This cannot be compared and calculated to arrive at a grand total of some kind. Perhaps, an argument can be made in favour of utilitarianism with respect to the avoidance of pain rather than positive promotion of happiness. In social and legal sphere it seems clear that policies and legislations are always introduced with a view to improving the lot of a large number of people and alleviate their suffering. For example, everyone will agree that better medical and educational facilities and penal code go a long way in promoting happiness indirectly by removing obstacles to a good life. But the variation in the quality of happiness and its connection with specific activity does seem to destroy the suitability of utility criterion as a clear guide to moral action. All the same it must be realized that in actual day-to-day life many of our judgments are governed by utilitarian criterion. Most people, when judging the merits of individual acts do seem to go for an assessment of the happiness or misery which could be produced by these acts. In a closed community or restricted circle people seem to have a general agreement on what kind of acts would produce what kinds of happiness or misery. They have a rough and ready way of assessing the consequences of actions involving other people. And they base their moral judgments upon these assessments. So, it is not possible to dislodge utilitarian principle from its operation in daily life. The utility principle seems to be specially favoured by those who have to make a decision on behalf of a collectivity and for the interest of a large number of people. Recently, in 1999, the British Prime Minister, Tony Blair in justifying NATO military action on Serbia in the Kosovo crisis, took a utilitarian position. He argued that when we consider the consequence of attacking Yugoslavia we find that certainly there is pain in store for all sides involved, namely, the Serbs, the Kosovo Albanians as well as the American fighters. But the consequence of not acting in this way has far more suffering in store for a much large group of people if we consider the long term consequence of allowing the Serbian Leader Slobadon Milochevich to get away with his murderous plan. In other words, weighing the consequence of acting or not acting in a certain way the governmental decision in question is reached and morally justified. All the same, from the above discussion it should be clear that in a large number of cases it will be impossible to employ the utilitarian criterion in any satisfactory manner. Moreover, as we shall see later on, the amazing complexity of moral life stops us from treating utility as the criterion of moral rightness of action.

Another major problem with utilitarianism is its justification by way of its derivation from its own version of human nature. By and large, the utilitarians uphold a form of naturalism. In naturalism, the standard of morality is derived from some characteristics of human nature which of course is supposed to be universal among men. The most famous argument in this regard was put forward by J. S. Mill. Mill claimed that all men by nature desire pleasure. What is desired in this way is, therefore, desirable because what is desired by each person is good to himself. So, the happiness of all, that is, the general happiness must be considered the moral good.

Various steps of the arguments relating to utilitarianism have been questioned. The most vehement attack on this form of naturalism came in this century from G.E. Moore. Moore claimed that Mill's argument involves a fallacy which can be termed as Naturalistic Fallacy. The fallacy, according to Moore, arises because the desirability of pleasure is identified or meant to have been derived from the fact that pleasure is actually desired. The former is a value statement which cannot be derived from a factual statement. In Moore's terminology, the desirability or moral goodness of something represents a "non-natural" property. While "desired" refers to a natural property. I would like to suggest that the so-called naturalistic fallacy is not a fallacy as such. A fallacy is a mistake in logical inference. But mill's argument has not made such a mistake if we put it in a syllogistic form, it would look like this :

(a) Pleasure is desired by all.
(b) What is desired by all is good to all.
(c) Therefore, Pleasure is good to all.

In the above mentioned argument the conclusion certainly follows from the premises. So what is wrong with this form of argument is that it is fallacious but that it blocks enquiry into what is good or the criterion of rightness. In moral philosophy we look for a justification of whatever criterion of rightness is suggested. The justification has to be independent of any assumption in this regard. We cannot take it for granted that what is actually desired by anyone must be good to him. Experience does not always uphold it. However, it seems to me that the ethics which recommends standards of choice, it would be clearly foolish to recommend to everyone to act contrary to what is universally desired by human nature. That is, if it were a fact that all men basically desire pleasure, then it seems to me that we would also have a natural inclination to consider pleasure as the most desirable end of human activity. I wish to point out that such characterization of human nature is incorrect. Moreover, as we have already noticed, the complexity of the concept of pleasure or happiness stops us from treating them as unitary ends. There are as many different pleasures as different forms of activities. With the added complexity of their differences in quality, the point is that there is no satisfactory account of human nature which could be generally agreed upon. Different versions of it have been proposed by different philosophers which lead us nowhere.

In any case, naturalism is not necessarily presupposed by utilitarianism. In fact, some utilitarians, most notably Sidgwick, have clearly disowned naturalism. In any case, it is only when the question of justification of the utilitarian standard is vague that naturalism comes into picture. Perhaps, it is not possible to give a strictly rational or logical justification of the utilitarian standards of morals, or for that matter, of any other standards of morals. Perhaps, the best justification of a standard of moral could be found in the actual act where people deploy it in their moral reasoning. If this be so, then, as we have noted earlier, we have the required justification since people do actually use the utility criterion in judging moral rightness of action.

However, it is equally clear that the utilitarian standard is not the sole criterion of rightness irrespective of whether it is taken in its hedonistic form or in its non-hedonistic form. There are clearly other ways of judging the rightness of an action without raising the question of its utility in promoting happiness such as judging an action by reference to a long cherished social ideal or religious belief. Bernard Williams argues that some of the unacceptable features of utilitarianism are there because of its general character as a form of consequentialism. Since in general, consequentialism is evaluation of moral value of any action in its consequences, it is by reference to their consequences that actions including institutions, laws and practices are to be justified whether they can be justified or not.[1] Thus, according to B. Williams, some undesirable characteristics of utilitarianism directly emerge from its general consequentialist structure. Other unacceptable features directly follow more specifically, from its purported alliance with the notion of happiness. He points out that two very important moral values, viz. justice and integrity cannot be adequately explained within the utilitarian structure of consequentialism.[2] Utilitarianism sometimes suggests that we should forget or ignore the value of integrity in favour of general good. Such suggestion, according to B. Williams, is wrong, since the reason why utilitarianism cannot accommodate integrity in its structure is because it cannot consistently explain the relations between a man's project and his action.[3] Robert L. Arrington is of the view that Mill's qualitative hedonism cannot be called a form of hedonism because according to him, pleasure can vary in quantity but not in quality. Thus, for him, it makes sense to talk of Bentham's hedonistic calculus to quantify pleasure. But he is skeptical of the argument that pleasures can be assessed as higher or lower than one another. His contention is that the pleasures of listening to classical music are different from the pleasures of drinking a good wine. Further, such pleasures are different from sexual pleasures or any other pleasures. But according to him, this is not to say that one type is superior in quality to others. Some of the so-called higher pleasures referred to by J.S. Mil like Socratic enjoyment in contemplation, cannot, in the strict sense be called as pleasures, since such enjoyments are not mere bodily sensations.[4]

Arrington further argues that :

> To measure the amount of pleasure or happiness produced by our actions is to apply the utilitarian standard. In the process of measuring the maximum happiness, it is easily conceivable that the question of merit can be completely ignored. In other words, while trying to maximize the overall utility, we need not necessarily treat people fairly. For example, an industrialist might cheat workers, in order to maximize profits and overall utility. But in such case, it would not be fair to cheat the workers. Similarly, in a cooperative enterprise, one who does not perform one's assigned duty, should not receive one's share of rewards, since one does not deserve it. But in the utilitarian scheme, lack of desert has little to do with an overall calculation of utility. Further, under utilitarianism, a society can benefit by punishing an innocent person. But punishing an innocent person under any circumstance is wrong, nay, highly unjust, since he (the innocent) does not deserve punishment. By punishing a petty thief severely, a greater utility can be achieved, but this will be at the expense of fair treatment.[5]

Further what the utilitarians do not explain is the process as to how an individual passes on from the psychological inclinations to that of moral obligation. In other words, the utilitarians appear to leave a gap between "is" and "ought".

Utilitarianism has also been criticised on the ground of possibility of conflict among various principles. The utilitarians offer a single and ultimate standard to take care of possible conflicts. Their moral standard referred to is that any action which produces the greatest happiness of the greatest number is the right one. But this principle contains within itself the question of distribution. The question of distribution in turn implies the concepts of utility and justice.

This type of conflict constitutes the most important moral conflicts that we face in human society. The fundamental moral question is : whose interest should be promoted at the expense of the other, when the interests of different people and groups are directly opposed to each other? For example, if stave-keeping is the practice of a society and by doing so, the greatest happiness of the greatest number is obtained then according to the utilitarian, the practice of slavery should be morally obligatory in that society. The utilitarians do not provide any answer to the conflict between utility and justice. In other words, the utilitarians cannot solve the major moral conflict between utility and justice in social life.

Furthermore, utilitarianism appears important in discharge of moral obligations particularly to our close relatives and friends. The utilitarian principle appears to advocate general impartiality towards all human beings. The moral problem in this respect is how do we maintain impartiality in our policy towards all human beings when most people instinctively feel greater sympathy towards their relatives, friends and fellow ethnic or racial groups compared to unknown millions all over the world. Perhaps, the standard reply would be that the stronger obligation towards one's close circles of relations and friends is justified because of the social utility implied in such special relationships. But if this is the foundation of true moral obligation to close circles or relations and friends, then it would also be right to break the natural ties and loyalty that we have with our close ones, as this will promote the greatest good for all human beings. The fact of our social life reveals that personal relationships and feelings determine morality for more than what the utilitarians propose. It seems to me that morality involves obligations and loyalty that we feel for our near and dear ones and also to override them for promotion of the greatest happiness of the greatest number. This is bound to generate more moral conflicts than it solves. Thus, it is clear that the theory of utility alone cannot provide the kind of measuring rod which will guide a person to evaluate which group of people should be counted and in what degree.

Autonomy of the Moral Agency

Utilitarianism is also criticized for the impartiality of its standard of rightness in undervaluing the moral significance of moral agent's commitments, projects and attachments. The utilitarian theory does not give importance to the relationship between an agent and his aims. According to utilitarianism, when one is judging an action, what is important is the impact of certain actions on the impersonal sum of utilities. Thus, the importance of the moral agency becomes very insignificant in such judgments, since the only reason for which an action is done is purely for the promotion of utility. In such a scheme, each individual's utility becomes a mere part of the sum total utility. The aim of moral conduct boils down to maximization of some utility total; thereby the importance of the moral agency is reduced to the utility carrier to the total stock of utility. Thus, a person is seen as a mere convenient instrument for creating utility; persons as such are not important but rather the utility they can produce.

It may be pointed out that human beings have some conception of good and it is this good which gives meaning and coherence to the various phases of our life. Perfect individuality is accomplished through identification of oneself with one's chosen goals and ends. However, from the utilitarian standpoint, individuality does not make much sense. Utilitarianism does not give due significance to personal commitments; it does not give meaning to an individual life. In actual life, it is utility or satisfaction which belongs to discrete individuals, whereas total utility is more of a computational convenience and as such it does not actually exist like the concrete happiness or pain of a person. So, it can be concluded from the above criticism that morality cannot be established on an impersonal foundation. It may be argued that for a moral standard, in order to serve as a sound basis for our actions has to give weight to the important relationship between the moral agent and his selected goals.

The utilitarian theory has been further criticized on the ground that if what one ought to do is guided by the only principle of utility then individuals having anti-social preferences like sadistic pleasures and the illiberal preferences can be justified in their actions on utilitarian principles or reasons. In spite of the major criticisms discussed above, utilitarianism does offer the broad outline of a theory of moral justification. It clearly views morality as a social institution in which the aim of morality is to promote and maximize the general human welfare and minimize pains and harms in human society. The moral rules and codes are meant to serve such purpose. The positive utilitarian contribution is that actions should be guided by their consequences for the welfare of the individuals. In other words, the individual well-being should be the motivational force behind our moral actions.

The utilitarian principle, i.e. the greatest happiness of the greatest number is an easily comprehensible ideal. But in real life situations, to implement this ideal in specific cases is very difficult because the consequences of actions are complex and vary from case to case. Each case needs to be judged individually with regard to its consequences. Some critics have pointed out that utilitarianism attempts to provide too comprehensive and extensive an answer to varied and complex personal and social problems to morality. According to them, it has provided only partial or unsatisfactory answers to moral problems. Lastly, unless the overriding quest for utility is controlled, other morally unacceptable conclusions and injustice may follow. The complexity of our moral life rules out a simple and universal way of arriving at moral judgments. From the above discussion we can conclude the following : Firstly, that though our moral life does provide a place for utilitarian consideration in moral reasoning, we cannot take the principle of utility to provide the sole criterion of rightness. Secondly, the notion of justification of the moral standard or principle is not clear-cut. Though naturalism does not entail utilitarianism, it does not mean that the principle of utility does not have same mind. Thirdly, the relative merits of the principle of utility *vis-à-vis* other principle vary from case to case.

This brings us to the second question we posed earlier, namely, the question "Can the consideration of the rightness of action in terms of utility be the sole purpose of moral evaluation?" But before I answer this question and the third question "Can moral philosophy of this kind capture the vast complexity of actual moral life?" I wish to consider the alternative to utilitarianism which is Intuitionism. This is because the above two questions are of general interest to Act Morality. The answers to these questions fix the common nature of the approach followed in moral philosophy of those theories which we have branded as Act Morality.

REFERENCES

1. J.J.C. Smart and Bernard Williams. *Utilitarianism for and Against*. Cambridge University Press, 1975, p. 79.
2. *Ibid.*, p. 82.
3. *Ibid.*, p. 100
4. Robert L. Arrington. *Western Ethics: An Historical Introduction*, Blackwell Publishers, 1998, p. 346.
5. *Ibid.*, pp. 350-51.

3

INTUITIONISM

Intuitionism is generally regarded as an alternative moral theory to naturalistic utilitarianism. It is radically opposed to naturalism because according to it evaluative statement in general and moral statements in particular are very different from factual statements. In other words, values cannot be defined in naturalistic terms, since values and facts are completely different from each other. Intuitionism has generally been advocated by rationalist philosophers. According to them, moral judgments are self-evident. We evaluate moral judgments with the help of rational intuition or immediate understanding.

Before I proceed to discuss the details of it, I wish to raise some questions : What kind of actions are good? Or what kind of actions should we perform? What state of affairs are good? What kind of things ought to exist for their own sake? According to G.E. Moore, the moral goods which ought to exist for their own sake are the intrinsic goods. But in this connection, a question may be raised as to how does one know what is intrinsically good. For an intuitionist like Moore the answer to such question is that one immediately recognizes the property of intrinsic goodness which one is faced with. For him, the intrinsic goodness as opposed to good as a means to something intrinsically good neither requires proof nor disproof. The reason for this is that good is the name of a simple, unanalyzable property. This non-natural property, according to Moore, cannot be identified with any natural property like red or pleasure.[1] Moore's clear distinction between natural property and non-natural property is very similar to David Hume's distinction between "is" and "ought". For Hume, moral statements cannot be derived from purely factual statements. If at all, it is possible, at least there should be one non-factual statement. In other words, evaluative conclusions cannot be derived purely from factual premises. There is a logical gap between facts and values and as such, evaluation or moral conclusion cannot be deduced from purely factual premises or statements. Humean arguments about the logical gap between facts and values which had been further developed by G.E. Moore in his *Principia Ethica* (1903) and became very important in modern moral philosophy. Moore has coined a new expression, 'Naturalistic Fallacy' which epitomizes distinction between facts and values like "is" and "ought". We have argued in the previous chapters that utilitarianism defines good in terms of natural property, i.e. like pleasure, human welfare, etc. A right action, according to utilitarianism, is that which can promote or bring about the happiness to the greatest number of people. Moore's attack is directed against this kind of naturalistic arguments. According to him, the naturalistic fallacy is committed when one attempts to define ethical terms like good, duty, right and wrong, and such others by terms that are purely factual or descriptive and, therefore, devoid of evaluative or moral force. For him, good can never be defined in terms of any other property, since it is simple, unanalyzable and non-natural property. Moral agents are either directly or indirectly aware of the good or they are not. Moore points out that the naturalists confuse between the two very different questions, that is, what is good and what kind of things are good. Such identification of two different questions is obviously fallacious for Moore since any such definition is bound to turn out an open or debatable question into a closed or trivial one. For example, if someone were to say that happiness is good one can still meaningfully ask whether happiness is really good. Even if one accepts that happiness is good still one is fully aware that the question is not without any significance. This is Moore's famous open-question argument.

Moore's open-question argument provides the background for the controversy in the contemporary ethical theory. It seems to me that his contention that good in ordinary language cannot be substituted for any naturalistic terms appears to be correct. However, most naturalists have rejected such contention because they argue that ethical terms like right, wrong, good and duty are vague, ambiguous and ill-defined words in ordinary language and, therefore, there is need for further clarification and even for revisionary definitions. Nevertheless, there is no denying the fact that the substituted meaning is not completely identical with the original meaning. But it is also a fact that such substitution of meaning gives us greater satisfaction for purpose of ethical theory.

Moore defines duty in terms of good but at the same time the apprehension of goodness is always a different step which is beyond the apprehension of the qualities of a thing. In his book *Ethics*, Moore argues that the apprehension of duty is very different from that of good and each is reducible to the other. For H.A. Prichard, the ultimate quality which cannot be analysed is that of duty. Mary Warnock points out that Prichard, unlike Moore, does not talk of logical fallacy in identifying obligatoriness with something elser ather one does not simply do it.[2]

What Ralph B. Perry and other naturalist admit is that G.E. Moore is correct in so far as what he says in the open-question argument. However, they go on to argue that it does not completely disprove naturalism. Moore's open-question argument at best shows that naturalistic definitions are not at all adequate but does not conclusively prove that naturalistic definitions are impossible. Further, it can be argued that it is impossible to define good taken in isolation.

But certainly good can be defined if used in certain context that has meanings dependent on it, for example, a good pen, a good house, a good person etc. though the concept of good as such cannot be defined.

Intuitionism is regarded as the most obvious alternative to naturalistic utilitarianism. Since intuitionism advocates that evaluative statements are not factual, and value predicates are not definable in naturalistic terms; it is radically opposed to naturalism as a whole. The intuitionists hold the view that moral judgments can be arrived at by the exercise or rational intuition or understanding. D. D. Raphael in his book *Moral Philosophy* points out that for the intuitionists there are many principles of right action. From among these several principles of right action, anyone can serve as the standard or criterion. Such principles, according to them, are self-evident, apprehended to be true by rational intuition. Intuition in this context does not stand for an inexplicable hunch. It is used in the sense of understanding.[3] The rationalist use the word 'intuition' for apprehension of self-evident truths in logic and mathematics. It also includes the self-evident necessity by means of which a conclusion follows necessarily from the premises of a deductive inference. Some intuitionists even apply the word intuition to the understanding of moral principles which is analogous to that of self-evident truths of logic and mathematics. But to say this does not mean that it is clear to every child, just as even we first become aware of the mathematical truths by teaching, similar is the case of our awareness of the moral principles, i.e. often it is not seen immediately that certain moral judgements are right. Once we have attained intellectual maturity of under-standing according to the intuitionists, we can see for ourselves that the normal principles are self-evidently true as pointed out by Raphael. Further, Raphael has brilliantly exposed the position or viewpoint of the intuitionists that the later attitude that we possess is not simply the result of conditioning. Because one does not come to consider as self-evident all the moral principles and rules have been taught to one by one's parents or by religious indoctrination. This is clearly seen from the fact that some of those rules change from one generation to another.[4] It seems to me that up to a certain extent, the contention of the intuitionists is correct. For example, we may argue that a particular action is wrong because it is a case of lying. One still raises the question as to why lying is wrong. We may reply by saying that lying is wrong because it causes unhappiness and obviously causing unhappiness is wrong. Similar examples such as promise breaking is wrong, stealing is wrong, killing innocent person is wrong etc. could be cited. In spite of the above examples, one may still genuinely raise the question as to which moral rules are the self-evident principles? In answer to the above question, D.D. Raphael has beautifully paraphrased the possible intuitionists' suggestion to all or most of the categories of action.

1. Promoting the happiness of other people.
2. Refraining from doing harm to other people.
3. Treating people justly (which might mean either (a) doing it in accordance with merit, or (b) treating them equally, or (c) treating them in accordance with their need).
4. Telling the truth or more accurately, refraining from deceit, for it would be an absurd imposition on other people and not a moral obligation to them to tell them every truth that we happen to know.
5. Keeping promise (including the fulfilment of contracts, e.g., the payment of debts, since the obligation to do so arises from promises).
6. Showing gratitude.
7. Promoting one's own happiness (prudence).
8. Maintaining and promoting one's own virtues (self-respect).

There is a certain lack of clarity in this list of what is alleged to be self-evident. Not all intuitions cite everyone of these principles or classify them in the same way.[5] Although there is no unanimity among the intuitionists on the details of their list of principles, they at least agree in their criticism of utilitarianism. According to them, the serious defect of utilitarianism is that it picks up a couple of most important principles and ignores the other principles. What utilitarianism picks up are those principles which have future consequences and neglects those principles which depend on the past. Some of the examples of those principles which depend on the past are promise keeping, gratitude and dispensation of justice in accordance with merit. Some of the examples of those principles which never depend on any point of telling time are equality, truth and justice.[6] For the intuitionists, certain moral judgments can be true without there being any empirical evidence in their favour. Intuitionism is a meta-ethical theory. In other words, it is a theory about the manner in which we get our moral knowledge. It relates to epistemology of morals. It tells us that we just intellectually apprehend, without any process of reasoning and ratiocination, that certain moral principles are necessarily true. Thus, according to intuitionism, we cannot argue for moral principles or give reasons for them.

But there is a need to clarify the confusion relating to intuitionism in this regard. Jonathan Harrison clearly points out that intuitionism as a moral theory is not a meta-ethical theory at all. Intuitionism is primarily concerned with what we ought to do, rather than with epistemological question of how we come to know what we ought to do. As we have said above, intuitionism is primarily concerned with rejection of utilitarianism. The utilitarians argue that there is one single supreme principle of morality. From this ultimate principle, all other moral principles can be deduced. In this sense, all other moral principles are derivative and subsidiary to the supreme principle of morality. According to utilitarianism, the single supreme principle of morality is that all moral agents ought to behave in such a manner as to bring about the greatest possible balance of good over evil. If utilitarianism as just defined holds the view that there is only one thing which is good, that is, pleasure or happiness, then such a theory is known as hedonistic utilitarianism. But if utilitarianism advocates that things other than pleasure like knowledge, aesthetic appreciation etc. can also be good, not merely because they are pleasurable or give rise to pleasant consequences but for something else, then such a view can be termed as ideal utilitarianism.[7]

In opposition to utilitarianism as stated above, intuitionism holds that moral properties are completely different from natural properties. According to it, value terms like duty, right, wrong, good, evil etc. do not refer to something that can be known through experience or through empirical verification. According to the intuitionists, things which are considered to be good have the property of goodness, but there is no way of knowing them empirically. Then the question arises as to what is this property of goodness? The intuitionists would argue that any proposition relating to good refers to a unique property, viz. goodness. Thus, whenever we say that something is good, we are simply ascribing some property to it. However, good is indefinable and unanalyzable, since it is simple. Value judgments can be either true or false depending upon the subject referred to as good or bad; whether they do or do not have the value property attached to them. But in this kind of statement, there is a logical difficulty involved, that is, if value judgments are not based upon factual evidence, how does one make out whether a value or ethical judgment is true or false? In response to it, the reply of the intuitionists is that basic value principles are known to be true or false by intuition or self-evidence only. There is a consensus among the intuitionists that there are different principles of right actions each of which can be used as the standard or criterion of one class of right actions. These principles are self-evident and are known immediately by rational intuition. For example, just as we intuitively know that if a triangle is equilateral, then it should be equiangular, similarly we come to know if something is good or bad. In the same way, promise keeping, debt-paying, truth-telling and so on, are known to be true. In other words, we directly apprehend the presence of moral property without taking the help of any sensory experience or empirical evidence. According to some intuitionists, we have a faculty or moral intuition and through this faculty we are able to apprehend moral truths. There are serious disagreements among the intuitionists regarding the states of certain moral principles since they classify these principles differently. For example, there are differences regarding the principles of truth-telling and promise-keeping. Some intuitionists argue that truth-telling is a form of promise keeping while others hold that truth-telling is more fundamental than promise-keeping. Regarding promotion of one's own happiness, some intuitionists argue that it is one's moral duty while others deny this except in certain situations where there is necessity to carry out actions that are considered as moral duties in themselves.

The intuitionists are one in their criticism of utilitarianism. They criticize the utilitarians of confining themselves with a principle which is solely concerned with the future and completely ignores those that concern with the past like promise, gratitude and justice according to merit. It seems to me that intuitionism is a theory on which anything can be justified including deep-seated prejudices. Far from providing a strong foundation on which moral beliefs could be founded or ultimately justified, intuitionism appears to move within its own circle, thereby treating mere opinion as if it were justified and true. It is because of this reason that the intuitionists are criticized by the utilitarians and others. It is true that moral judgments are generally reached in ordinary life in the manner the intuitionists argue, yet many philosophers would argue that it is not enough for an adequate moral theory. Therefore, there are certain serious and important objections against the intuitionist theory.

According to the intuitionists, value principles are self-evident. However, the serious disagreement and the ambiguity that result from the different accounts of some of the principles, clearly demonstrate that they are not as self-evident as it is claimed. And as the intuitionists raise objections against the naturalist beliefs in natural moral properties which they consider as absolutely indefensible, they (the intuitionists) advocate the possibility of non-natural objective property which is known by rational intuition. However, it seems to me that there is no such evidence that moral discourse refers to such properties, let alone there being evidences that they exist. Here the difficulty is not because of our inability to discover the property of goodness through sensory experience of it. It is the impossibility of having no means to find the so-called simple moral properties at all, much less to find them objectively, and it is precisely this reason which makes it difficult to accept the claim that such properties exist.

Further, the claim of the intuitionists that they know something to be the case is itself very vague and highly ambiguous because to claim that one knows something is not only to state that something is true and believed but also that one knows how to justify the claim. There can be various ways of justifying a knowledge claim. But the intuitionist's only means of knowing something is intuition itself. Intuition without the support of other methods or means appears to be a matter of mere belief. Therefore, if one is not in a position to demonstrate that an intuition is something very different from mere belief, then one is not entitled to the knowledge claim so fundamental to intuitionism.

Intuitionism does not have the answer to the problems of moral disagreement, where justification is indispensable.

Thus, intuitionism cannot resolve the conflict between two or more principles. In such a situation, one person's intuition appears as good or bad as that of the other. At least, for utilitarianism, whenever moral rules conflict with one another, it can be resolved by resorting to alternative principle which can provide the greatest utility in promoting general happiness. But, utilitarianism as seen earlier has also its own severe constraints.

Intuitionism has been criticized on the ground that it fails to provide the self-evidence required of a moral principle. Intuitionism is also criticized on ground of actual conflict of principles. Utilitarianism, on the other hand, provides a ready solution by offering a single fundamental standard to resolve such conflicts by upholding that the action which produces the greatest happiness of the greatest number is the right one. But this principle leads to the question of distribution of happiness which is very important to any moral theory. Further, the question of distribution leads to the concepts of both utility and justice. Conflicts between these two concepts very often constitute most of the moral conflicts that arise in human relationship. The moral question frequently arises as to whose satisfaction should be promoted when the interest of different people, classes, and grcups are directly in conflict with one another? In such a situation, the most difficult and common case is conflict among various interest groups such that it so happens that one group is benefited only at the expense of the other.

Another objection to intuitionism is Moore's account of "good". According to Moore, "good" is the name of a simple, unanalyzable non-natural property which we just simply recognize by our rational intuition. But this view does not explain anything. His account leaves it entirely unexplained and inexplicable as to why something being good should ever provide us with a reason for action. It is argued that any account of good which is to be sufficient must have some close connection with action and explain why to consider something good is always to give a reason for acting in respect of it in one way rather than another. According to some intuitionists, apprehension of something as a duty is said to be immediate and unquestionable and as such, it need not be supported by reasons. Alasdair MacIntyre has his own serious objection to intuitionism. He argues :

> Prichard's outstanding characteristic, and one which he shares with Moore as well as with other intuitionists, is the treatment of good, right, duty, obligation, and the rest of the moral vocabulary as though it was a coinage of permanently fixed values and simple scrutiny. It is doubtless because of this that the proportion of assertion to argument is so high in Prichard. In other intuitionist writers, such as Sir David Ross, who holds that we have independent intuitions or "rightness" and "goodness" the standards of argument are much higher. But all intuitionist writers suffer from one difficulty they are, on their own view, telling us only about what we all know already. That they sometimes disagree about what it is that we all know already only makes them less boring at the cost of making them even less convincing.[8]

MacIntyre further points out that in his perception the two most powerful critics of intuitionism were R. G. Collingwood and A. J. Ayer. According to MacIntyre, the main criticism of Collingwood is the lack of historical sense in intuitionism. And the intuitionists have the tendency to treat Plato, Kant and themselves as contributions to the single discussion with a single subject matter along with a permanent and unchanging moral vocabulary. A.J. Ayer in his book *Language, Truth and Logic*, classifies propositions in terms of a threefold classification, namely logical, factual and emotive. The truths of logic and mathematics which are analytic come under the first class. The empirically verifiable or falsifiable truths of sciences and of common sense knowledge of fact come under the second class; within the third class, come ethics and theology.[9] The self-evident principle of the intuitionists is very much subject to uncertainty since there is doubt and disagreement about their nature and among different cultures at different times and places. Therefore, it is not unambiguously self-evident.

It seems to me that the claim of intuitionism in comparing our knowledge of moral principles to our knowledge of axioms of mathematics is naïve and simplistic because moral judgment or propositions are not like mathematical propositions. For example, the statements that promise-breaking is wrong or lying is wrong do not have the same status as the proposition if a triangle is equilateral then it must be equiangular or two plus two equals to four. In the case of mathematical proposition, we cannot say that five plus five is ten is true at some place but false at other. Further, we cannot say that five plus five is ten is true at some time and false at another, true when asserted by some individuals, false when asserted by others. Given a particular definitions of certain mathematical terms and within that fixed definitions, if a mathematical proposition is true at all, it should be true everywhere and at all times and in all societies. It is never the case that five plus five is ten is true in India, but false in China or true today, but was false five thousand years ago, or is true when stated by a prophet but false when stated by a layman. As I mentioned earlier, similar case is not obtainable with regard to moral propositions. As a matter of fact, in certain societies polygamy is considered right but considered wrong in other societies. Similarly, patricide is wrong in many societies but it is right in the north of Arctic circle. In the same way infanticide and slavery are considered wrong at the present time but were considered right before many, many years ago. The response of the intuitionist to the above objections is that the same moral principles when applied to different circumstances, tell people to do different things. Therefore, according to them, the so-called apparent differences of moral principles are not at the core different from each other. Jonathan Harrison explains the intuitionist answer to the difficulty or objections raised above in the following words :

> Owing to the different circumstances which obtain at different places and at different times, an action can actually be right at one place and time, and another similar action actually be wrong if performed at a different place or at a different time, and then proceeds to explain that the same moral principles applied to different circumstances enjoin different actions. The principle that one ought to drive safely, for example, will enjoin in driving on the left-hand side of the road in England, but on the right hand side of the road in the United States. The second answer says that, owing to different people or groups having varying opinions on matters of fact, they may think that moral principles, which they both accept, enjoin different actions in circumstances which, though they suppose them to be different, are in fact the same.[10]

It seems to me that up to a certain point, the argument of the intuitionists is correct because it is quite possible that the same moral principle can produce a difference of opinion about what one should do as people's beliefs about the situations to which they are applied are not in fact different in any significant way. One can also point out that the circumstances to which moral principles are applied, differ from place to place and from time to time, thereby we have different duties at those times and places. For example, there may be no moral disagreement between the doctor who recommends that a patient should have an operation and another doctor who recommends that the same patient be given drugs. The difference in what they think they should do is not because of disagreement over moral principles but because of a different assessment of the factual situation to which these moral principles are to be applied. In the same way, even at the level of human society there may not be any moral dis-agreement between a community which considers cannibalism with moral abhorrence and another where cannibalism is prescribed as a duty. In this situation, it is quite possible that both communities accept the same moral principle but the different conclusions they reach in what they do in particular circumstances may be because of a difference of opinion on a matter of fact. One community may regard eating the flesh of one's enemies as a duty, may be influenced by the belief that by doing so one assimilates their virtues to oneself, whereas another community may bury them, may be being influenced by another belief. Thus, the same moral principle may give rise to a difference of opinion as to what one ought to do.

Having considered the answers provided by the intuitionists to some of the objections or difficulties to their theory, the next question that comes to my mind is that different actions in different circumstances are performed merely because of the differences on matter of fact alone. Secondly, is not there genuine disagreement on moral principles? The claim of the intuitionists is that if different people have the same belief on matters of fact, they will agree with one another on questions of moral principle. It seems to me that such claim is too simplistic and naïve as to overlook the serious numerous differences of moral principles people hold. The fact that there are several moral theories available in the history of moral philosophy is an ample testimony to the genuine differences of moral principles people hold and it is not because of different assessment of matter of fact. For example, a Christian missionary may not agree that killing elderly relatives is right even if he or she is convinced that keeping them alive will reduce their mobility, and the chances of survival of their tribe. It can also be argued that a highly educated European woman may not approve of polygamy practised by certain societies, even if those societies consider that wives are a great financial asset.

From the above consideration it is clear that people genuinely do disagree over moral principles. It is also not possible to explain away all apparent disagreements over questions of moral principle as being due to people holding the same moral principles but drawing different conclusions from them solely because of differences of opinions on matter of fact. In spite of these criticisms, the intuitionists try to justify their contention by citing the examples of mathematics that sometimes we think we can grasp truths which we do not in fact grasp. Sometimes, we are under the impression that what we grasp is true but we do not clearly grasp the necessity of its truth or what we think we apprehend is not even true. In the same way, the intuitionists argue that similar misapprehension of moral truths takes place. Though what we intuit must be true but this does not mean that we may sometimes appear to intuit that which is false. According to the intuitionists, temporary misapprehension is possible but skepticism is impossible. Even the demand for proof of the truth of ultimate moral intuitions is unnecessary, nay non-sensical, as the demand for proof in the case of genuine knowledge. Once one has got a moral intuition, it is impossible to doubt what is that one has; and anything in terms of which one tries to prove its truth would be necessarily less true or certain than the intuition itself because according to the intuitionists, particularly to Prichard when one knows something one always and necessarily knows also but one knows it. One can never be mistaken when one comes across something that one knows. According to Prichard, genuine knowledge has a kind of trade mark such that it is impossible to mistake it for other thing.[11] Thus, the claim of the intuitionists particularly that of Moore is that we human beings have a capacity for direct, perception—like insight into the presence of the non-natural simple and unanalyzable property of goodness. By saying that goodness is non-natural what Moore is claiming is that goodness is not reducible to any property that is scientifically observable. His contention is that this moral feature is non-natural by demonstrating that all theories that attempt to equate it with natural feature of the world are bound to commit a fallacy, that is, the Naturalistic Fallacy. To identify goodness with something else, such as pleasure is to commit a fallacy. The notions of right and duty are not derivatives from ideas of good. As seen earlier, W.D. Ross argues that we are capable of being directly and immediately aware of certain rules of obligation what are binding on us. H.A. Prichard emphatically argues that duty and right cannot be a function of self-interest or the ends of desire.

Although the intuitionists claim the veracity of direct and immediate awareness of moral principles yet their claim is not absolute in all cases of moral principles. Thus, intuitionism can be said to have lost all its dash. Their claim of immediate awareness of moral truths is highly diluted. One has to be very careful in stating that moral principles hardly serve us as guide at all. Mary Warnock points out that the relativity of moral principles is to be assessed by grading principles in order of self-evidence. According to Ross, there are some principles which are completely self-evident. For example, the principle that we should produce as much good as we can. Mary Warnock opines that W.D. Ross does not mean to suggest that even this principle can never conflict with any other. Ross, according to Warnock, maintains that it might conflict with the principle of keeping promises. Even the top-grade principles are likely to conflict with other principles. Mary argues that such principles are not likely to be very helpful.[12] It seems to me that Mary's argument is very logical and gives a death blow to the basic claims of intuitionism itself. Further, she goes on to explain :

> The second grade is made up of those principles which can be derived from the first by reference to general truths about human nature; the third grade is of principles derived from the first reference to the particular circumstances which obtain in any given period or place; the fourth and last grade is of principles wrongly derived from the first by reference to false opinions about human nature.[13]

From the above discussion it appears that some moral judgments are *a priori* and some are synthetic. The first grade of moral principles make it appear as if our knowledge of morality is *a priori*. In other words, when we have collected all the necessary facts about a person or a state of affairs, it appears that we do not require to collect any more facts in order to make moral assessment. Furthermore, it does at least appear as if moral judgments, if true, must be necessarily true. For example, the right and proper way of behaving is to try to bring into existence the maximum amount of human happiness. It seems to me that there are many cases where something may appear to be right and proper way of behaving but it may so happen that this is not the proper way to behave when more detailed account of the situation in which the action has to be performed has been collected. There are many things which are right and proper to do in some circumstances but which are not necessarily proper and right things to do if circumstances are different. Therefore, it cannot be necessarily the case that such and such is the right and proper way of behaving, since it is just a contingent fact that circumstances are as they are.

Such difficulty, according to the intuitionists, applies only to derivative moral judgments and not to the ultimate principles of morality. A derivative moral principle is always derived from some ultimate moral principle by mediation of some factual proposition. It is the factual proposition which provides the necessary promise on the basis of which deduction of the derivative from the ultimate principle is made possible. For example, from the fact that we ought to act in such a way as to maximize happiness, we can derive that we ought to keep our promises, provided it is the case that keeping own's promise does in fact, maximize happiness. And keeping one's promises is a contingent fact. Although the intuitionists' attempt to show that there is no contingency in ultimate moral principles, but this is not so. According to me, all the principles of morals are contingent, that is why, we have so much moral chaos and confusion. Further, it seems to me that human beings since the time of recorded and known history have not advanced morally in a significant way. And this is ample testimony against the necessity of the first grade moral principles.

It seems to me that intuitionism as a moral theory can hardly provide guidance to what is right or wrong. It seeks to provide a solution to the problem of how we know what things are right and what things are wrong. To say that we know moral judgments to be true by intuition does not really do more than inventing a shield to hide our ignorance. To state that we know moral judgments to be true by intuition is simply to say that we know them, but this is to refuse to explain how it is that we do know them to be true. Such assertion without attempting to give any reason or rationale of such knowledge, is completely too crude a method of dealing with the problem. As such, this kind of theory fails to capture the vast complexity of actual moral life. In the next chapter, I wish to consider the arch rival to utilitarianism that is Kantianism. To reiterate, intuitionism is concerned with epistemological issues relating to morals and moral values but it does not offer any solution to the problem of what we should do. In other words, intuitionism cannot help us in exercising moral choice.

REFERENCES

1. Alasdair MacIntyre. *A Short History of Ethics*, Routledge and Kegan Paul, 1993, p. 249.

2. Mary Warnock. *Ethics Since 1900.* Oxford University Press, 1960, pp. 56-60.
3. D. D. Raphael. *Moral Philosophy.* London : Oxford University Press, 1984, p. 43.
4. *Ibid.*
5. *Ibid.*, p. 44.
6. *Ibid.*, pp. 44-45.
7. Jonathan Harrison. *Our Knowledge of Right and Wrong.* George Allen & Unwin Ltd., London, 1971, pp. 74-75.
8. Alasdair MacIntyre. *A Short History of Ethics.* Routledge and Kegan Paul Ltd., 1993, p. 254.
9. *Ibid.*, p. 255.
10. Jonathan Harrison. *Our Knowledge of Right and Wrong.* London, George Allen & Unwin Ltd., 1971. pp. 79-80.
11. Mary Warnock. *Ethics Since 1900.* Oxford : Oxford University Press, 1960, p. 61.
12. *Ibid.*, p. 72.
13. *Ibid.*, pp. 72-73.

4

KANTIANISM

Before I begin my discussion on Kant, I would like to raise the following questions :

1. Can Good Will or Good Intention be a criterion or only criterion of rightness of action?
2. Can the consideration of the rightness of good will or good intention be sufficient for moral evaluation?
3. To what extent, Kantian moral philosophy can capture the complexity of moral life?
4. Could Kant's universalizability principle be a criterion of morality if not the sole criterion?
5. Do we not in real life actually use Kant's principle?
6. What is the standard of morality?

Kant advocates a moral standard which is termed as the universalizability principle. It is a kind of non-naturalism. Kant is anti-naturalist. His moral theory is an attempt to place ethics on a strong foundation, that is reason. We have already seen that, the utilitarian moral theory in attempting to provide a single standard, had failed to provide a unified and coherent account. For example, *Justice* a very important aspect of moral life is left out by utilitarians. According to utilitarianism, moral value of actions is judged by its capacity to produce good consequences by maximizing greatest good of the greatest number. In contrast to such argument, Kant argues that actions are right and good if they conform to moral principles. According to Kant, moral standards are independent of utilitarian goals. In other words, consequences do not matter in moral evaluation and that actions are right or wrong in accordance with their conformity or non-conformity to the relevant moral rules or principle.

What is Kant's conception of moral duty? Different moral theories have their principles of duty as the final moral standard. According to Kant, the moral value of actions can be known only through reason. He attempts to provide an important basis, that is, a rational basis from which all other moral principles, rules and other judgments could be derived.

In this chapter, I shall attempt to present Kant's rationalistic argument to provide a foundation of morality. I shall bring out a general survey of the important characteristics of Kant's rationalistic ethical theory and evaluate whether such approach to morality is adequate in demonstrating that ethics can be founded on reason. In other words, I will examine if a rationalistic foundation can be given to ethics. According to Kant, the nature of human agency forms the background of understanding morality. The peculiar characteristic of human agency is our capacity to act on the basis of reasons. We humans can conceptualize our ends or goals and act so as to bring certain things to fulfilment. For Kant, such a capacity is peculiar only to human beings as rational creatures. Thus, for him, moral acts are guided by reason which identifies the goal of the action and frames its own moral rule or principle for achieving it. These moral rules framed by practical reasoning act as rational constraints against our inclination to action irrationally.

Kant in his book, *The Groundwork of the Metaphysics of Morals,* tries to find out and establish the ultimate principle of morality thereby to show that all human beings as moral agents are subject to this. Thus, for him, the universal basis of morality is possible because of the rational nature of humans. Our reason provides the *a priori* foundation of morality. In other words, the ultimate principle of morality can be known *a priori*, that is, independent of experience. The fundamental principle of morality constitutes the necessary condition for objective moral knowledge since it is the direct outcome of the human capacity for practical reason. Our whole moral reasoning revolves round the way we ought to behave. Further, our moral life is an aspiration to be fulfilled by a whole range of standards, models or ideals of perfection none of which is found in the world of pure theoretical experience. Since moral obligations are binding on all conceivable rational agents, by logical implication, moral implications can never depend fundamentally on the feelings, desires and inclinations that we humans happen to have. It also follows that for Kant moral obligations should be independent for moral agent's subjective make-up and beliefs. Further, they should be fully objective in being the same for all rational agents. Thus, for him, reason is the basis of moral knowledge and rightness is objectively determined by it and the situation is the same for all rational agents placed in similar conditions. According to Kant, conformity to reason is one of the basic pre-conditions of morality. For him, reason is objective and impartial thereby there is logical consistency in it. The truths produced by reason are necessary and universal in application to all rational agents. Without objectivity, moral obligations would carry no authority and knowledge. And without impartiality, there would be partisanship which may be termed as caprice and as such cannot guide human conduct at all. For him, an action is moral if and only if there is purely a moral motive behind it. And the only pure motive is the good will to all actions because it is right or obligatory as determined by practical reasons.

For Kant, *good will* is the highest good, a good without any qualification. It is good will which represents the efforts of a rational agent to do what he ought to do, rather than to act from one's desires or inclinations. MacIntyre has beautifully paraphrased Kant's conception of the good will.

> Kant approaches this question from intuitional assertion that nothing is unconditionally good — except good will. Health, wealth and intellect, are good only in so far as they are used well.[1] But the good will is good it "shines forth like a precious jewel",[2] even if "through the niggardly provision of a step motherly nature."[3]

The agent is insufficiently strong, rich, or clever to bring about desirable states of affairs. Attention is thus focused, from the outset, on the agent's will, on his motives and intentions, rather than upon what he actually does. What motives or intentions make the good will good?

The only motive of good will is to do its duty for the sake of doing its duty. Whatever it intends to do, it intends because it is its duty. A man may do what is, in fact, his duty from quite other motives. A shopkeeper giving the correct change may be honest not because it is his duty to be honest but because honesty pays by bringing his customers and thereby increasing his profit. But it is important to note here that a will can fail to be good not only because duty may be done from selfish motives but also because duty may be done from altruistic motives which nonetheless spring from inclination. If I am a friendly, cheerful and kind person by nature who enjoys helping others, my altruistic acts, which may be, what duty in fact demands from me, may be done not because duty demands them but just because I have an inclination to behave in this way. I enjoy it. If so my will fails to be decisively good, just, as if, I had acted from self-interest. Kant rarely mentions and never dwells upon the difference between inclinations to act in one way rather than another; the whole contrast is between duty on the one hand, and inclination of every kind on the other.[4] MacIntyre points out that for Kant, inclination is part of the physical and psychological nature, therefore, in Kant's view one cannot choose one's inclination.

What one can do is to choose between one's inclination and one's duty. Duty is obedience to law and that is universally binding on all rational beings. The Kantian moral duty as MacIntyre points out is a set of precepts which can be prescribed to all rational beings without any exception. The test of the genuineness of the moral imperative is its character of universalizability. In other words, one can will this so that it becomes a universal law. Since consistency is part of rationality in law, moral agents prescribe these laws to them as rational beings.[5] The example of this precept for Kant would be promise keeping among other things. According to Kant, promise-keeping should be universalizable consistently otherwise it cannot be called categorical imperative. Kant has contrasted the categorical imperative with hypothetical imperative. A categorical imperative is not limited by any condition. Whereas a hypothetical imperative is limited by certain conditions. For example, if one wants to be successful, one ought to work hard. One ought to do such and such if one wishes to be happy. As mentioned earlier, a categorical imperative is limited by no condition. It can assume the form: you ought to do such and such because it is your moral duty. Thus, the categorical imperative commands us to be good irrespective of any reward. But in this context, we have the age old conflict between duty and self-interest. The advocates of duty argue that there must be a categorical imperative or a supreme *a priori* principle being the fundamental principle of the autonomy of reason of action which is in the direction of high level abstraction. While those who advocate self-interest argue that there are only hypothetical imperative that is, do such and such if you want to gain this or that. The conflict involved here is whether a rational being like man can perform moral duty without some kind of incentive. Can there be some sort of incentive which can be termed as moral?

Can a complete rational consideration be adequate to determine the will to action? Is it necessary to supply an incentive that is adequate for performing an action? Purely rational considerations are *a priori*, that is, they are completely independent of experience. Rational action is different from unintentional or automatic motion. This conception can be formulated as a rule or maxim which can be either categorical or hypothetical. If the maxim is categorical then the action is purely determined *a priori*. But if the maxim is hypothetical, then the action is empirically determined. To act on a categorical imperative means the same as not acting on some empirical conditions. For example, a person tells the truth even if telling a lie might promote his well-being and success. Moral concepts require an individual to act solely from respect for the moral law. And this universal law is meant for the sake of a self-regulating community of the kingdom of ends. Not one of these categorical imperatives of maxims can be sufficiently exemplified in experience and, therefore, they all must be *a priori* conception.

As long as the categorical imperative provides criteria for determining what is to be done by pointing out an end or a rule or an incentive, it is a practical principle. But this principle cannot decide about moral character. Thus, any overt action which is contrary to lawfulness is bound to be unjust. It is also morally wrong because it could not have been done for any morally acceptable reason. Therefore, any action which is unjust and morally wrong is hereby blameworthy.

As we have seen earlier, Kant forcefully argues that there is absolutely no possibility of thinking anything at all in the world which can be regarded as good without qualification except the good will. Intelligence, with judgment, courage, resolution, perseverance etc. are doubtless in many respects, good and desirable. Nevertheless, they can also become extremely bad and harmful if the will, which is to make use of these talents of the mind and heart is not good. Similarly, with gifts of fortune like power, riches, honour, health, complete well-being and contentment can also become extremely bad and harmful unless there is a good will. Therefore, a pure and good will seems to constitute the indispensable condition of being even worthy of happiness and right action.[6] Some qualities are conducive to such good will and can facilitate its work. But Kant argues that such qualities do not have intrinsic unconditional worth. He says :

> They always presuppose, rather, a good will which restricts the high esteem in which they are otherwise rightly held, and does not permit them to be regarded as absolutely good. Moderation in emotions and passions, self-control, and calm deliberation are not only good in many respects but even seems to constitute part of the intrinsic worth of a person. But they are far from being rightly called good without qualification (however unconditionally they were comprehended by the ancients). For without the principle of a good will, they can become extremely bad; the coolness of a villain makes him not only much more dangerous but also immediately more abominable in our eyes than he would have been regarded by us without it.[7]

It is clear from the above argument that the good will is good not because of anything but because of willing in the light of reason. It is good in itself like a jewel which shines by its own light as something which has its full value in itself. Nothing can either augment or diminish this value. In other words, its usefulness or fruitlessness can never be altered by any external influence. To act from good will is also to act solely from a sense of duty, and such action has got only genuine moral worth. When there is discontent with one's condition under so many pressing problems then, deep unsatisfied wants may easily lead to a great temptation to transgress one's duties. Further, when the strongest and deepest inclination towards happiness and pleasure comes directly in opposition to the principle of good will, whether the rational beings can obey the universal law of duty is highly doubtful. According to Kant, in order to achieve unconditioned and moral worth, one's action should be determined by the formal principle of volition. For him :

> Duty is necessity of an action done out of respect for the law. I can indeed have an inclination for an object as the effect of my proposed action, but I can never have respect for such an object, just because it is merely an effect and it is not an activity of the will. Similarly, I can have no respect for inclination as such, whether my own or that of another.[8]

A true object of respect can only be one's will solely as ground and never as effect which does not serve one's inclination rather excludes it completely. Since the law itself can be an object of respect as such it is a command. In other words, an action done from the sense of duty must completely exclude the influence of inclination and incentive. But it seems to me that such rigorous demand of duty by *a priori* principle for the majority of rational being is an almost impossible thing. Since there is an eternal struggle between duty and inclination in man, I wonder, if the Kantian moral theory is workable or practicable in our day-to-day life. It seems to me that the Kantian duty may turn out to be a vain delusion and a chimerical concept.

Roger K. Sullivan points out that Kant himself acknowledges the fact that the human moral condition is in a state of constant inner conflict between two warring elements. On the one hand, the unyielding demands of *Duty* and on the other, the instinctive lure of temptations against those demands are always in conflict. In fact, it is because of such ongoing endless struggle that we become aware of the reality and nature of morality. Thus, according to Sullivan, Kant himself is not aware of the opposition between the subjective pressing desires and the rational and objective ideal of what one ought to do.[9] Further, he contends that for Kant, the fact that rational beings are self-conscious, therefore, they are capable of being aware that their moral obligations claim their obedience in a categorical manner. The categorical or law like character of moral obligation for Kant, demonstrates the objective nature of morality.[10] The formal criterion that Kant has offered has the characteristics which is such that anyone who accepts it as his own should consistently desire that everyone else should make it one's principle of conduct. They ought to involve here directly what arises from the moral, that is the good will informed by reason. A categorical imperative is an unconditional command which is derived from Reason itself and it is applicable to every experience. In other words, it has reference not to what is but to what ought to be. For Kant, the highest moral guide is the pure practical reason and its norm; the categorical imperative. According to Kant, to argue that there is some authority like God/Society beyond the individual's own moral reasoning, will destroy autonomy and with it, morality. To attribute the whole responsibility of moral decision to the autonomous judgment of the moral agent presupposes that each person can know what is right and what is wrong.

Three Variations of the Categorical Imperative

Kant explicitly argues that there is only one categorical imperative but he gives three formulations of it. The first formulation is to do with the form of the categorical imperative; the second is about its content and the third links the two together. Kant's three formulations of the categorical imperative are :

1. Always act on a maxim which can become a universal law of nature. In other words, act as if one were legislating for every human being.
2. Always act so as to treat every human being as an end and never merely as a means.
3. Always act as if one were a member of a possible kingdom of ends.

The above formulations or prescriptions are meant to avoid partiality. In other words, one is to treat one's decision as if it were a law for everyone to follow.[11] The categorical imperative has the form of a universal prescription. We can paraphrase Kant's formulation of the categorical imperative so as to consider one's proposed action as if it were a natural occurrence according to a law of nature.

D.D. Raphael points out that for Kant, there is nothing wrong with treating a person as a means so long as one does not treat him merely as a means like treating a slave. Each member of human beings should treat all the others as moral beings. One has to respect their desires, allows them freedom of decision and also should recognized that everyone can and should decide as if legislating for all. There is the element of universality of moral decision to the fact that moral decision treats people as ends. Such respect for others desires and freedom of decision implies a form of equality for all men. It also implies that every human being has the power to make choice and decision, including moral decision binding all moral agents. From the above argument, it is clear that Kantian theory of ethics embodies liberty, equality and fraternity.[12] Kant's formulation of the categorical imperative is confined to the treatment of human beings only and says nothing about the treatment of non-human creatures. This is because of Kant's emphasis on the importance of rationality in ethics. Kant assumes that non-human animals do not have enough rational capacity to take independent decisions, therefore, it follows that it is not morally required to treat an animal as an end.

D.D. Raphael seems to think that Kant must have been influenced by normal moral consciousness exhibited by most people, because most human beings do not think it immoral to use animals merely as means when they are killed for food. Raphael argues that Kant's categorical imperatives is an explicit account of normal human moral consciousness. Therefore, it must lack the refined moral sensitivity of few exceptional saints. Today, quite a lot of people are skeptical about the ethics of killing animals for food. Peter Singer is one among the few leading campaigners of animal rights. In the light of this, D.D. Raphael suggests that Kant's second formulation of the categorical imperative which provides the content should be extended to animals as well.

> Act so as to treat rational and sensitive beings as ends and not merely as means. This will mean that we have respect for the desires of animals and we do not unnecessarily cause pain to them unless for a more important moral purpose. Such treatment will still consider human beings as more important than other animals because such treatment considers other animals as ends in a more limited sense.[13]

Kant's notion of the Kingdom of ends arises because he believes that rational human beings are unique and irreplaceable, each one having an incommensurable value as an end-in-one-self. It is only in living the moral live can we participate with dignity in the kingdom of ends. Perhaps the general philosophical ground for preferring empiricism to rationalism may offer a definite advantage over Kant's position in explaining why we have moral obligations to non-human as well as to human animals. It seems to me that Kant's injunction to view one another as rational and autonomous ends-in-themselves is highly laudable and profound. The fact that we do not extend our love, compassion and respect to other sentient beings like the non-human animals, is limited in scope. Perhaps inadequacy of Kant's moral philosophy is partly because of the argument that to act morally is to act from a sense of duty and not from inclination. It seems to me that spontaneous compassion for the suffering of other rational sentient beings is a kind of inclination which is morally good. Buddha and Mahavira have acknowledged such compassion as part of morality. On the contrary, Kant maintains that happiness is best achieved through a life of instinct and that reason, far from promoting happiness, is often an obstacle to it. Reason can induce doubt and uncertainty. Reason can lead to an estrangement from the emotional life. It can be dry and not nourishing. Reason may give little contentment and happiness. Yet Kant's view of Morality is based on reason, despite little promise of pleasure and happiness.

Autonomy and Heteronomy

If our action is caused by any external situation and other agents then we can be said to be acting heteronomously. In other words, if our act is coerced, manipulated and controlled by any external agent other than ourselves, there we do not act autonomously. Even when we choose to be motivated by our own inclinations, we are acting heteronomously, because our inclinations are external to our rational self. For Kant, the rational self has to bring its own actions. When reason guides the will and impose its own law on it, then such act is autonomous. Therefore, for Kant, to act morally is equivalent to acting from a sense of duty. And to act from a sense of duty is to act autonomously.[14]

Kant is fully aware of the constant struggle between moral life and feeling of emotions, desires and drives. In other words, the struggle is between the 'is' and the 'ought' that is; what we want to do is seldom the same as what we ought to do. If our actions are to have moral worth, duty should motivate them and not inclination like that of Aristotle, Kant's understanding of human nature is essentially rational and moral although he does not deny that we are at the same time creatures of desires and feeling. There is a logical link between Kant's emphasis on autonomy and his emphasis on the freedom of rational and moral aspects of the human person.[15] Robert L. Arrington points out that Kant himself is fully aware of the many extremely difficult questions relating to his moral theory based on autonomy and reason. Firstly, can a moral agent guide Himself by reason? Secondly, can one obey the command of the moral law in the face of severe competition and opposition from the forces of desires, drives and feeling? Lastly, can one act from free will? Kant argues that free will and free action are presuppositions of morality. He emphatically argues that "ought" implies "can". At the same time, Kant is also very sensitive to the possibility that human will and action are causally determined. Further, he is also painfully aware of the philosophical thesis that inclinations are the cause of all human actions and even inclinations are caused by either physiological conditions or external events which are beyond our control.[16] Arrington points out that universal determinism was widely prevalent in Kant's time and Kant himself being a believer in Newtonian mechanics, must have had an extreme theoretical puzzlement in putting forward his moral theory. In the light of this, certain seriously disturbing questions come to mind :

1. Can we be moral?
2. If morality depends on autonomy, how is morality possible?
3. How is the categorical imperative possible?

Kant having meticulously attempted in his Groundwork to establish the basic principles and presuppositions of morality, finally wonders whether he has described an illusion. Arrington argues that :

> Perhaps we are unable to be guided by reason in such a fashion as to obey universal laws, to treat one another as ends, and to act autonomously. Perhaps the kingdom of ends is an idle dream incapable of being realized.[17]

It seems to me that Arrington's observation is very insightful because Kant himself was acutely aware of the serious problem of human freedom which is reflected in the *Critique of Pure Reason* while dealing the metaphysical and epistemological aspects of thought.

The Postulates of Immortality of Soul, God and Freedom

Kant argues that one's duty is one's duty irrespective of the consequences whether here on the earth or in the next world. But at the same time, he argues that life would be unbearable and miserable if duty were not ultimately rewarded. In this respect, Kantian notion of happiness is different from any notion of socially established ends and the satisfaction to be derived from achieving such ends. Kant can hardly be said to be consistent here in introducing happiness as the reward of virtue. In order to be consistent, he has to maintain that even if there is reward of virtue, the reward is not primarily sought after by the moral agent. In other words, it can be said that there is the reward of virtue only if it is unsought. But such a stand, MacIntyre points out, amounts to a tacit admission that without some such notion the whole enterprise of morality would scarcely make any sense. Thus practical reason presupposes for Kant a belief in the existence of God, immorality of soul and freedom.[18] The human will is powerless to ensure that nature will allot the happiness deserved by the virtuous. But the moral law upholds a necessary link between virtue and happiness. Therefore, the coincidence of happiness with morality leads to a perfect being like God. In other words, the existence of God is postulate because of the need to ensure happiness for moral agents. In the ultimate analysis, happiness is a very important part of Kantian ethical theory. But happiness is not the basis of the moral law nor it is the supreme principle of the law. On the contrary, happiness is grounded on the moral law.[19] Thus the existence of God is to ensure the guarantor of the fact that the virtuous will attain happiness. Immorality of the soul is postulate because virtue and happiness do not usually go together in this world. Further, the complete fulfilment of the will to the moral law is a kind of perfection which no human being is capable of attaining in this world. Therefore, practical necessity demands that there should be endless progress to that complete fitness of the will to the moral law. And such endless progress is possible only under the presupposition of an infinitely lasting existence and personally of the same rational agent which is the immortal soul. In other words, the highest good is practically possible under the assumption of the immorality of the soul.[20] Lastly, as we have seen earlier, freedom is the presupposition of the categorical imperative. For, it is only when our acts are in conformity with the categorical imperative that we can be said to be free from the bondage of our own inclination.

An Evaluation of Kant's Moral Philosophy

Kant's idea of an unconditional good will of good motive is absolutely essential for human conduct and evaluating human acts. The absolute good will is opposed to evil deeds and conduct. Therefore, when its maxims are made into universal laws, they can never be contradictory. Kant's supreme principle or law is this: Always act on a maxim which you can, at the same time, turn it to a universal law. This rule alone guarantees consistency, impartiality and objectivity to will and so is a categorical imperative—the supreme law of the absolutely good will. Secondly, Kant's treatment of every rational being as an end, or the maxim always act according to a principle which is universally valid for every rational being is highly laudable and praiseworthy. We wholeheartedly approve of Kant's argument that no act is good without some qualification that it has its source in a good motive or a good will. Thirdly, another very important merit of Kant's moral theory is that to live by reason is to be consistent, rather than to live by mere drives, desires, impulses and inclinations which lead to inconsistency. Kant is to be commended for emphasizing rationality and the use of reason in the formulation of moral judgment. To respect the worth of all rational beings is a very sound principle in line with what we as human beings expect from other fellow beings in interpersonal relationship.

Having seen the points of strength in Kant's moral theory, let us now identify certain weaknesses and problems in it. It seems to me that the categorical imperative is not adequate as a moral guide. A critical examination will demonstrate that Kant's rational account of morality does not provide an adequate basis for morality. According to Kant, in order to evaluate whether our act is moral or not is to be judged from the motive should be one of acting from moral principles. If one acts with expectation of some reward or some other consideration, then such action will not have any moral virtue. Kant's emphasis on motive seems proper but too much emphasis on moral principle alone can be too narrow. For example, if a person were to save the life of a drowning man or woman, being moved to do so merely by compassion, would amount to an act which will be morally indifferent. It seems to me that just doing what the principles require is not good enough since all principles are not worth acting on, as quite a lot of cruel dictators have been persons of principle. In other words, there should be some value to be added to one's principle as moral content.

Hegel sharply disagrees with Kant when the latter asserts that the moral motivation should abstract itself completely from all incentives of inclinations thereby the moral agent can act on the principle of duty for duty sake absolutely and not at all from the slightest inclination. According to Kant, some actions may be in agreement with duty but if they are performed from feeling of love, loyalty, friendship, pity, generosity or some other end then they lack moral worth although they themselves may be good. Hegel does not agree with such Kantian view because for Hegel, the motive for duty may sometimes require the cooperation of sensuous inclination and with the involvement of inclination in the duty, does not in any way take away the moral worth. In general, Hegel contends that Kantian moral principle does not provide any determinate moral guidance when one is faced with practical moral situation. Therefore, Kant's categorical imperative and universal law are too general, formal and empty of content. This raises the question concerning the scope of morality. It is clear that Kant's philosophy limits the scope very radically. Therefore, it is reductive, though it may have captured one dimension of ethics quite successfully.[21]

Further, Hegel argues that Kant's sharp division or the divorce between reason and inclination is unrealistic because for Hegel, Kant's strict enforcement of control of the empirical self by the rational self is a very unhealthy and unnatural form of self-alienation. Hegel advocates a kind of harmony between reason and inclination. An essay by Xavier Mao submitted to the University of Sydney (1996, p. 10, unpublished) and sense like the one advocated by the ancient Greek philosophers.[22] Kant's recommendation to lawfulness and universality alone cannot guide us to the idea of any specific actions being treated as our duty. When an individual acts from valuing whatever factor provides the principle a moral content, like a person who, out of compassionate feeling, acts towards someone, he is said to be acting out of compassion. In this example, one values the compassionate act and further in such act there is no desire for reward or the impact of any extraneous motive. In such a situation, Kant is committing a mistake since according to him, we must not act from bad or neutral motivation, rather we should act from obedience to principle itself and nothing else except that. My contention is that compassion can give the principle the moral content which Kant has ignored.

Hegel has criticized Kant's concept of absolute rules embodied in his categorical imperative since the command of absolute rules completely neglects the important consequences of our action. In real life situation, this is not the case. For instance, in a situation where promised-keeping would result in a person's being seriously hurt or even killed. Kant has not answer. In a situation such as this, Kant is criticized on the ground that he provides very little solution as to how to resolve conflicts, whether to keep a promise or prevent an innocent person from being injured? The dilemma is real. On the one hand, we have a duty not to kill or injure and on the other, a duty not to break promise. Such conflict is between conflicting duties; whether to obey mutually opposing but equally categorical imperatives. Kant did not consider the virtues like pity, love, generosity, loyalty friendship etc. which may be termed as independent moral values, since he rules out mixed motives as sources of moral actions. It seems to me that any act done out of complete willingness is a better act than the act done from Kantian notion of a strong sense of duty.

Kant has also been criticized for being inconsistent in his account of morality. As per Kant's theory, many rules of questionable moral values can universalized without inconsistency. Kant also argues that a particular rule cannot be morally universalized, since such a rule will be counter-productive for the person who is saying it. Here, Kant implicitly implies that consequences of such a rule is bad. This is inconsistent on his part since his moral theory disregards consequences. In other words, absolute rules, and not the consequences are the basis of morality. In agreement with Hegel, I am inclined to argue that we cannot conceive of any moral theory which is not concerned with consequences at all. Any moral theory is to do good for oneself and for others. Whatever be the kind of moral system, moral prescriptions of each theory are calculated to provide some good consequences for the greatest number possible, if not all human beings and other sentient beings. If we simply adopt Kant's non-consequentialist theory we thereby exclude many other theories. In solving real life conflict situation, to arrive at good answers is very crucial and difficult but subscribing to absolutism along like Kant's principle, would be disastrous in any moral system. Further, ethics cannot be simply spinned out of *a priori* reason on the spot. Some acts have to be right before we meaningfully ask which principles are right.

A good volition must define both in terms of content and form. Therefore, Kant's attempt to provide a fundamental ethical principle does not fulfil this condition. Kant's theory excludes the performance of unique acts in certain specific circumstances. His theory suggests uniformity in good actions. The richly varied manifestation of moral life cannot be easily captured by the kind of uniformity Kant's theory suggests. Thus, his theory has serious limitations in providing a sound foundation to morality as his theory of goodness consists in conveying universally applicable rules. Despite the shortcomings, Kant's view that a rational agent should treat others as ends-in-themselves, and others should never be treated as mere means has definite advantage over consequentialist theory like utilitarianism. His account of rationality has the merit of recognizing the person as having primary moral significance. Accordance to me, the proper moral realm should be found within our interacting community of persons where different individuals have their varied desires, interests and inclinations. Acting morally is not merely obeying the absolute principles. Kant, by laying too much emphasis on universal applicability of moral rules, has neglected the question of what and where the interests of other moral agents lie and then there is the important question of which interests should take priority over other interests. Morality is not just all about recognizing other human moral agents as having moral standing and treating them respectfully but also to recognize that other people really do count morally. It is very good to have Kant's recommendation of the right principles and rules to guide us, nevertheless, we still require to possess a good attitude towards other moral agents; an attitude of love, care, respect, sharing and considering interest, and well-being of others. Further, his recommendation to treat other people as ends-in-themselves logically implies that others should be treated with respect. But it does not strictly follow from the purely formal principle of universalizability of one's maxim of action which the categorical imperative demands. To treat other people with respect is important but Kant has not successfully substantiated how it could be achieved from rationality alone. Our moral behaviour should embrace the diverse interests of people since such interests are vital and important to them. Our moral theory should also reflect which interests should take precedence over other interest and so on. Kant's view that our rationality alone gives us moral significance is too narrow, since human moral agents are very complex beings with varied qualities of rationality, spirituality, emotion, sentiments, etc. Thus an adequate moral theory should concern itself with interest and well-being of all of us taking into account the varied aspects of human life.

REFERENCES

1. MacIntyre, A. *A short History of Ethics,* London : Routledge, 192.
2. *Ibid.*
3. *Ibid.*
4. *Ibid.*
5. *Ibid.*, p. 193.
6. *Grounding for the Metaphysics of Morals*, p. 7.
7. *Ibid.*

8. *Ibid.*, p. 13.
9. Roger J. Sullivan. *Immanuel Kant's Moral Theory*, p.5.
10. *Ibid.*
11. D. D. Raphael. *Moral Philosophy*, pp. 55-56.
12. *Ibid.*, p.57.
13. *Ibid.*, p.58.
14. Robert L. Arrington, *Western Ethics*, p. 281.
15. *Ibid.*
16. *Ibid.*
17. *Ibid.*
18. *Ibid.*
19. *Ibid.*, p. 292.
20. *Ibid.*, pp. 291-292.
21. *Hegel on Kant and Morality*. An essay by Xavier Mao submitted to the University of Sydney, 1996 (Unpublished).
22. *Ibid.*

5

THE SCOPE AND LIMITS OF ACT MORALITY

We are not in a position as yet to consider the ventures of Act Morality and come to definite conclusions about its scope and limits. In discussing the two major approaches to moral judgments we have seen that both types of theories aim at providing only one standard by reference to which it is expected that one could judge the rightness of all actual or possible actions. The availability of such a standard should help any moral agent in making up his mind to choose between alternatives. A given moral standard is then, seen to be the only correct standard as well as universally applicable one. So far we have seen that the utilitarian and the Kantian standards both are employed in actual life in judging the merits of certain possible or actual action. This shows that neither is an exclusive standard. We have also seen that each is more suitable than the other in certain types of situation. In other words, none of the standards of morality suggested in act morality can be treated as the sole criterion of moral rightness.

There seems to be a number of assumptions behind any moral theory of Act Morality. Variety: (1) The claim of exclusivity of a suggested moral standard seems to presuppose the idea that in the variety of different types of cases the rightness of whatever is proposed as action consists in the presence or absence of some one particular quality or attribute in the action. For example, its pleasure producing quality or its quality of rational derivation from the categorical imperative is regarded as the standard. (2) The claim of universal application of a proposed moral standard seems to presuppose that moral life is homogeneous that there are no internal contradiction or conflict. (3) It also presupposes the internal rationality of moral phenomenon. (4) The whole approach seems to presuppose that the moral agent is perenially placed in a situation of exercising choice. In other words, the whole business of morality consists in choosing between the alternative courses of action in a given situation. (5) Further, Act Morality presupposes that the whole business of ethics is to judge action in respect of their rightness or wrongness. In other words, it presupposes that moral qualities pertain primarily to actions only. To other things, they apply only in a derivative sense. (6) Finally, the whole approach of Act Morality seems to presuppose that the tremendous variety and complexity of actual moral life can be reduced to a simple paradigm embodied in the situation of choice. In other words, there are no 'area of darkness', as it were, in moral life. Let us consider all these presuppositions in some detail between the rise or fall of Act Morality depends upon whether or not they can be justified.

When we look at the actual moral situation, it is abundantly clear that there is a kind of pluralism in respect of moral quality of action aimed at, that is, in acting morally, the qualities or effects which moral agents hope to realize in their actions are of many types. Thus, to relieve the suffering of others is said to be useful because it promotes happiness but dying for truth as Socrates did, does not seem to be obviously connected with promotion of happiness. In fact, if Socrates had lived, his admirers and perhaps the society at large, would have felt happier. Similar thing can be said about Jesus who accepted the crucifixion on the cross. Nor does it have anything to do with the quality of universalizability invoked by Kant. The Socratic action is not right because everyone ought to do the same in the similar situations. We call Socrates right, it seems to me, because we admire a character which stands for the truth even at the cost of one's life. This leads us to the second presupposition mentioned above. We tend to think that one moral recommendation cannot conflict with another and if it does then there must be a way of establishing the superiority of one over the other. But again, in real life this does not seem to be the case. We know that in actual life moral dilemmas abound. A moral dilemma exists for the moral agent when in a given situation one or more different courses of action present themselves as duties; each appears to be equally important but the moral agent cannot perform all of them together. He has to choose one of them. In such a situation surely whatever quality determines one's choice alternative course of action. Though the moral agent is guided by some background cannot be ruled out in determining his choice. Moreover, moral life does not seem to be homogeneous in the sense that often moral thinking leads one to a blind alley; the moral agent is confused even though he knows the standard norm of his society. He is unable to see the right answer. This is not because one is incapable of thinking rationally but because of the nature of the problem one is facing. This is not surprising since life cannot always be put in a straight-jacket.

The third presupposition mentioned above concerns the internal rationality of moral phenomenon. In the recent times, R.M. Hare has been the champion of the call of the rationality in the nature of moral argument. He maintains that moral judgments are prescriptive. By this, he means that the major function of making a moral judgment is practical in the sense that it prescribes a course of action. A moral prescription is not subjective as the emotivists have mentioned rather it is based on reason. If one is asked to justify one's prescription one would refer to the principle of choice involving some property which one considers morally commendable. If in turn, one is asked to justify the so-called justification one would conduct a similar exercise. In this way, the justification of a moral prescription is a rational process leading ultimately to a principle for which no further justification can be given. Hare argues that one's ultimate principle generates a way of life based on ordered principles constituting an inter-related system. The system as a whole is internally free of inconsistency and is based ultimately on one's *choice* of the ultimate principle. Now it is not difficult to see that even if such a system of morality is allowed to be internally consistent, it could not be held to be 'rational' if it is ultimately based on one's choice which is itself without reason. The whole edifice of justification seems to collapse if ultimately one's moral life considered as a whole is a matter of one's own choice. It is this problem which has led the existentialist to deny rationality of morality at all. The existentialists emphasize the contingency and the uniqueness of each individual situation of which the moral agent finds himself. According to this view, values are brought into the world by human choices. Given thus, the nature of values and the uniqueness of Moral situation, the existentialists leave no room for rationality in morals. It seems to me that both R. M. Hare and the existentialists capture some truth about moral life. But neither of them can be regarded to be wholly acceptable. As we noted earlier, in actual moral life, there are indeed situations which are unique and no prescription of moral action can be rationally produced for the purpose. But this is not true always and in every case. We indeed argue about reasons and try to be consistent with our other choices. However, this element of rationality in morals does not cover the whole of moral life. Often arguments break down, debates become interminable, and what justifies one position does not seem to have any logical relation with what justifies another position. Again, we might say that there are areas of darkness within the light of reason illuminating the moral life.

Another objection of Act Morality concerns the way they visualize human situation. Morality of course is about how people ought to live *together*. Living together means constant interaction with one another, that is to say that life in a society is a web of relationship. All forms of relationship are open to moral consideration, since people are related to each other though their feeling, intention and attitude as well as their overt responses to each other. But the Act Moralists imagine the moral agent to be perennially placed in the situation of choice where his actions alone are the proper objects of moral evaluation. This seems to be a limited view of the matter. Some virtue ethicians have made much of this point and condemn Act Morality as a proper approach to moral theory. It does seem to me too, that in the normal day-to-day life, we are not always *choosing* as such between the alternatives as it were. In normal circumstances, we relate to others naturally and quite spontaneously from the background of our individual character and personality. Life will be impossible to live if we had constantly to choose and deliberate before doing anything at all.

The above mentioned point is obviously connected with the idea that the focus of Act Morality is upon the evaluation of individual acts. For this theory, moral quality pertains primarily to acts. To other things such as the moral agents and their motives, moral quality apply only indirectly. It is this act-centered structure of modern moral theories that has come heavily under fire from virtue ethicians. Thus, *In Quandaries and Virtues: Against Reducitivism in Ethics,* Edmund Pincoffs says :

> The structure known as ethical theories are more threats to moral sanity and balance than instrument for their attainment. They have these malign characteristics principle because they are, by nature, reductive. They restrict and warp moral reflection by their insistence that moral considerations related in some hierarchical order.[1]

Pincoffs goes on to argue that the theories of Act Morality are "standard moral theories" foundational in the sense that the standards of moral evaluation which these theories prescribe are derived from some or other aspects of moral experience which are regarded to be absolute. Thus, Pincoffs points out that deontologism in general, especially Kantianism, emphasises the 'formal rectitude of the will' while utilitarianism emphasises the distributive Maximization of good consequences of actions. Such theories, Pincoffs calls "reductive". They are reductive in the sense that all types and varieties of ethical standards are reduced to a single overriding paradigm. The assessment of moral action is then made in terms of its satisfaction of the paradigm only.

In his approach Pincoffs argues that there are two major defects which affect Act Morality. Firstly, the reduction of moral concern to a single paradigm has the consequence of ignoring the rich variety of human moral life and its language of moral assessment. It is easily forgotten that we make moral assessment not only of human action but also persons and social practices. And when we assess persons and practices, the language of assessment which is employed has often nothing to do with their chosen paradigm; the moral rectitude of the will or the maximization of human happiness etc. The standard moral theories, according to Pincoffs, relegate the assessment, for example, of our character and of the virtues and vices of others, to the periphery declaring them to be secondary and derivative from the primary assessment of actions. They are led to treat these assessments as secondary because they do not neatly fit into their chosen paradigm. That is, such assessment resists being compressed into a dominant problematic. Clearly, when we assess persons and their choices, we do not try to ascertain something more than whether the choice has been made according to the principle of universalizability or the principle of maximization of happiness or any other principle considered to be the sole and decisive factors of morality of an action. For example, if a woman is choosing a man for marriage she does not reason with herself according to the principle of unversalizability because the considerations of mutual love and commitment to the other is a very personal and individual matter which cannot be fitted into a universal principle nor does her choice of a person as husband has anything to do with maximization of general happiness. A person of a certain character who honours his commitment and personal love will not even try to deliberate on his choice of marriage partner to whom he feels committed by virtue of his standing friendship. This shows that moral life in all its richness and complexity cannot be reduced to a single problematic. This aspect of the irreducibility of moral life has been very successfully demonstrated by Bernard Williams as well. Williams has shown that in assessing persons and their character, we employ notions which he calls 'thick' moral notions such as treachery, brutality and courage. Such aspects of human character cannot be brought under the reductivist scheme exemplifying a single overriding moral principle.[2]

This connects with the second point which Pincoffs makes. He calls the standard moral theories "quandary ethics". In quandary Ethics, moral understanding is exhibited in the moment of decision-making in which the moral agent follows the procedure of applying his chosen supreme principle to particular cases. If he judges correctly according to this principle, he is supposed to have captured the morality of the case accurately. In other words, it is held that practical rationality is best exhibited when the moral agent faces a quandary and gets out of it by applying a rule of action. But Pincoffs argues that in this approach, moral reflection is considerably limited and often gets distorted. This is so, because the kind of quandary and the person who finds himself in it, in the first place, already shows his character and moral insight. The point is that the right kind of action flows quite naturally and spontaneously from the right kind of character requiring no prior deliberation in particular cases.[3] A similar point has been made by Russell Hittinger in the following example :

> An agent who is seriously inclined to, and who actually deliberates about, marital infidelity might make the 'correct' decision according to rules advocated by one or another theory, yet the correctness of the decision does not alleviate, and indeed can obscure, the specifically moral dimension of the quandary. We can imagine, for example, a professor who returns from an academic conference and confesses to his wife that although he felt strongly urged to commit a marital infidelity, he deliberated about the moral significance of the action and concluded that it was violation of the golden rule (if he is deontologist), or perhaps that he came to his sense and saw that such an action would not bring about the greatest good for the greatest number (if he is a utilitarian). None of us would blame his spouse if she were as much or more concerned with the man's character than with the fact that he successfully resolved a quandary according to rule.[4]

The point here is again that assessment of person and their character is important for ethics and undue concentration on the moral of decision-making procedure undermines the importance of such assessment by treating them as derivative from the assessment of the rightness of actions.

We are now in a position to take an overall view of the whole approach of Act Morality. The question we are posing now is whether the Act Morality or what Pincoffs has called quandary ethics, is the right way of doing moral philosophy or the shortcoming of this approach requires abandoning it altogether bringing something different in its place. In the first place, we must recognize the richness and the complexity of actual moral life. Any judgment in a way of doing moral philosophy must be sensitive to its needs of capturing the essential features of this complexity. The complexity is reflected in the language which we use in making moral judgment. This language is not always only about the rightness and wrongness of actual or possible action. This language reflects the kind of gradation in terms of the acceptability and permissibility of acts. Such evaluation cannot be arrived at by a straight-jacket application of a single moral principle.

Moreover, the language of moral evaluation is often about person that takes into account character of persons and their world of inter-subjective relationship. It is clear that the goodness or otherwise of a person as a whole cannot be derived from the rightness of a few actions which one may happen to perform. Thus, whether or not goodness is more fundamental than rightness, it is certainly a very significant feature in determination of the overall character of moral life. And obviously, these features of morality are not taken care of by Act Morality. Similarly, moral judgments concerning the inter-subjective world of a moral community has nothing to do with treating individual moral choices as it would have done if Act Morality were the all comprehensive approach to morality. For example, in a marriage relationship, a woman would naturally attach much value to how her husband thinks and feels about her. She would naturally expect a loving disposition from him. She may naturally expect fidelity from him. Now one can make a moral judgment about her expectations. One may say, for example, that it is wrong for her to expect absolute fidelity undermining the strength of the nature of the man predisposed to a certain degree of promiscuity. Or one may argue that this expectation is wrong because it is a curtailment of the husband's essential freedom. And such evaluation, obviously are not matters of choice according to a supreme moral principle.

Furthermore, in Act Morality, the moral agent is treated as an anonymous agent equipped with the pure abstract will and moral rules. He is then to face the world thus equipped, and interact with other similar anonymous agents. This type of characterization of the moral agent and his situation seems to be very unrealistic. Moral agents are not mere wills but people with certain character traits, aims and ambitions; they are thus, equipped with the whole personality which must interfere with the rules which they are to follow. Moreover, in day-to-day life, one's actions are not really chosen in the strict sense of the word. In the normal course, action flow quite naturally from the psychological background of our whole personality without prior deliberation. It is only rarely that we are faced with a quandary needing to be settled by exercise of choice.

Next, there seems to be kinds of acts which are not amenable to the evaluative categories of standard moral theories. This point has been made well by Hudson :

> One of the recognized blemishes of modern moral philosophy, one that has recently been addressed, had been the tendency of moral philosophers to classify voluntary actions (or kinds of actions) under three headings : (1) Acts that are duties, or obligatory, or required, or that we ought to perform, these terms and expressions being treated as synonymous; (2) Actions that are forbidden, that we have a duty or an obligation not to do from which we are required to refrain; and (3) Actions that are permissible, in the sense that they are neither obligatory nor forbidden. Two sound lines of criticism have been advanced against this improvised list of moral categories. Let us review each.

> Call these categories (respectively) the morally obligatory, the morally prohibited, and the morally indifferent. Are they adequate for capturing moral reality. No supererogatory acts exist. A soldier uses his body to shield his comrades from a hail of bullets, a neighbour rushes into the burning house to save his friend's child. These are acts of supererogation: Often characterized as 'above and beyond the call of duty'. Such acts cannot be accommodated in an adequate manner by the categorical trinity. They certainly do not belong to the category of the morally obligatory nor to the morally prohibited. But it is misleading in extremes to place such acts in the category of the morally indifferent. Surely, some morally favourable characterization should apply; these acts are not morally indifferent in the manner that, say, chewing bubble gum on the way to the stores is.[5]

Another problem with this classification is that it is baneful and obscurantist.

> Recall that the morally obligatory is construed as a general classification that applies to actions (or kinds of actions) that are duties, or obligatory, or required, or that we ought to perform. And this is a mistake, these terms are not synonymous. If they were, then a statement like 'I ought not to fulfil my promise even though I am under a moral obligation to do so', should be baffling gap because it is self-contradictory. But such statements are coherent. And at times, true. There are times when promises are to be broken and there are moral grounds for doing so. They are the rule, of course, but no matter.[6]

All the same, there seems to be some other types of acts which must be judged in the manner of Act Morality. I am thinking of especially the acts of Corporate Bodies in which no single individual can be held responsible. In such acts, it seems to me that their rightness or wrongness can be determined only by reference to their overall contribution not only to the good of the organization but to the good of the community as a whole in which they exist. But again, if the primary question of ethics is, how should one live together with other people? Then it is clear that Act Morality may be charged with for not addressing the question at all or at least directly. This is so because living together with other people considered in its totality could not be simply a matter of making string of choices.

In all these above mentioned ways the scope of Act Morality appears to be limited. It is this perception which, as we noted earlier, leads Pincoffs to term Act Morality as quandary ethics. The important objection to Act Morality from this quarter is that standard moral theories take one or other aspect of moral experience to be absolute and fundamental. Their fundamental principles are then based on their chosen fundamental aspect. We have accepted Pincoffs' objection that this approach leads to reductivism. That is, we accept the view that the complexity of moral life cannot be reduced to a single paradigm. But do all these shortcomings in the approach of Act Morality confirm the view that we should bury it altogether? I have already suggested that this need not be done. There are occasions when we must approach the situation with a determination to choose one way or the other. In such a situation, we can only rely on the approach of Act Morality, if we are to avoid subjectivity in morals. In other words, while the charge of reductivism is valid, the Act Morality can be vindicated if it is limited to special situation I mentioned above.

This is not to say that all is well with Act Morality. A more serious problem which comes to my mind refers to the fact of plurality of fundamental principles. Even Pincoffs' objection recognizes the fact that standard moral theories capture one or the other important aspect of moral experience and the fundamental principles embody these aspects. The objection, therefore, is not that Act Morality does not represent something important about morality but that it treats one or the other aspect as the fundamental. The problem here then, is that all these fundamental principles, though justified in their own right, cannot be ordered within a single unified scheme of principle. In other words, we do not have an ordinatio of moral principle embodying more significant values of moral life. By 'ordinatio' is meant that impersonal and objective truth by reference to which we can adjudicate between the relative merits of the said fundamental values of moral life. Only if we have an ordinatio of this kind that we could hope to succeed in the approach of Act Morality. In the absence of such ordinatio, we are left with only a limited value of the standard moral theory. Can we replace Act Morality with Virtue Ethics? Can Virtue Ethics remedy the shortcomings of Act Morality? In the following chapters, we proceed to answer these questions.

REFERENCES

1. Edmund L. Pincoffs. *Quandaries and Virtues: Agent Reductivism in Ethics.* Lawrence: University Press of Kansas, 1986, p. 3.
2. Bernard Williams. *Ethics and the Limits of Philosophy.* Cambridge : Harvard University Press, 1985, pp. 140, 143-45.
3. I owe this point to Prof. M. M. Agrawal in discussion.
4. *International Philosophical Quarterly,*Fordham University, No. 4, December 1989, pp.145-452.
5. Stephen D. Hudson. *Human Character and Morality,* Routledge & Kegan Paul, Boston, London and Hurlly, 1986, pp. 28-29.
6. *Ibid.,* pp. 29-30.

6

THE CHARACTER OF VIRTUE ETHICS

Earlier in the introduction, I have already noted that the variety of theories in the name of Virtue Ethics have cropped up in moral philosophy to take the place of supposedly failed theories of Act Morality. I have also put forth certain claims which seem to be common to all the theories of Virtue Ethics. It is now time to examine some of these theories to see if they can sustain their claims and succeed in providing new directions to moral philosophy sharply distinct from Act Morality.

The primary theory in this context is obviously that of MacIntyre who is considered as the pioneer in this field. MacIntyre is of the view that contemporary moral philosophy has become paralysed and such theories have reached a number of dead ends. Moral debates have become "interminable". According to MacIntyre, the beginning of the problem in contemporary ethical thought can be traced back to the Enlightenment when with the advent of new secular scientific rationality moral philosophers said good bye to Aristotle. He contends that until then, by and large, ethics was based on the Aristotelian view (with a theological gloss in the middle ages) of moral agency which was teleological. The Enlightenment broke away from that tradition. And since then, there has been a gradual decline in the number of the proponents of the teleological ethics in general and of the teleological conception of moral agency in particular.

> The diversity of contemporary moral debate and its interminability are indeed mirrored in the controversies of analytical moral philosophers. But if those who claim to be able to formulate principles on which rational moral agent sought to agree, cannot secure agreement on the formulation of those principles from their colleagues who share their basic philosophical purpose and method, there is once again *prima facie* evidence that their project has failed, even before we have examined their particular contentions and conclusions.[1]

He goes on to compare their attempts to make sense of the left-over moral vocabulary of the middle ages with an imaginary attempt to make sense of the eighteenth century Polynesian use of the word *Taboo* which being wrenched away from its historical context had lost its meaning. These philosophers, he says, take it for granted that our moral rules and practices are in "good order" where in fact, they have been "fragmented" and thrown into disorder. Being unable to understand the historical and social changes which have stripped off the meaning from the words *good, right, obligatory,* etc., they want to explain the modern uses of these words in content-neutral terms. For G.E. Moore, for example, 'good' denotes a simple non-natural property. For the emotivists, like C.L. Stevenson, it has descriptive meaning but is used to stir emotion in others. For the 'prescriptivists' like R.M. Hare, again these words have no positive content but are used to recommend to others what one has chosen for oneself. Such theories of persuasive use of ethical terms do not show sensitivity to the fact that these moral terms have lost their ethical content in historical transitions to a new context, and therefore, the elucidation of their current uses and usages cannot capture the truth about ethics. MacIntyre sums up this point in his diagnosis of the failure in question as follows :

> Up to the present in everyday discourse the habit of speaking of moral judgments as true or false persists; but the question of what it is in virtue of which a particular moral judgment is true or false has come to lack any clear answer. That this should be so is perfectly intelligible if the historical hypothesis which I have sketched is true : that moral judgments are linguistic survivals from the practices of classical theism which I have lost the context provided by these practices. In that context moral judgments were at once hypothetical and categorical in form. They were hypothetical inso far as they expressed a judgment as to what conduct would be teleologically appropriate for a human being : 'you ought to do so-and-so, if and since your telos is such-and-such' or perhaps 'you ought to do so-and-so, if you do not want your essential desires to be frustrated'. They were categorical in so far as they reported the contents of the universal law commanded by God : 'You ought to do so-and-so : that is what God's law enjoins'. But take away from them that in virtue of which they were hypothetical and that in virtue of which they were categorical and what are they? Moral judgments lose any clear status and the sentences which express them in a parallel way lose any undebatable meaning. Such sentences become available as forms of expressions for an emotivist self which lacking the guidance of the context in which they were originally at home has lost its linguistic as well as its practical way in the world.[2]

In effect, the emotivist claims that there is no rational argument for an objective foundation of morals, and, therefore, moral judgments are made only to manipulate others through their emotion, are correct. Indeed, for MacIntyre, 'emotivism has become embodied in our culture'. It is against this background that MacIntyre's own Virtue Ethics get a foothold in moral philosophy.

MacIntyre and others have made attempt to rescue and to recover the so-called "common Morality" of the West (as in Alan Donagon's book *Morality*). The virtue ethicians are heavily impressed by the fact of ethical pluralism, both in the real life and in moral philosophy. They reject the approach that attempts to reduce the richness and variety of ethical life to a single overriding problematic. The common remedy which they prescribe is a call for a return to the ethics whose central concept is that of 'Virtue'. This involves the shift of the focus of ethics away from problematics or quandary towards character; — away from Hobbes and towards Aristotle. But this shift is to be made without invoking the traditional notion of essential human nature and a telos fixed by the essence of man.

In his book *After Virtue*, MacIntyre points out that virtues are neither atomistic nor amorphous values. According to him, virtues are qualities which constitute the character of a pesson. Firstly, it requires to teleological scheme which connects the conception of "man as he is" with the conception of "man as he might become where his telos are fulfilled."[3] He argues that without a teleological scheme, the conception of virtues will find no place in moral theories, since virtue, apart from being good in themselves as meant basically to enable man to attain his telos. In modern moral theories discussions on virtues were found unnecessary just because philosophers did not subscribe to a teleological theory of nature and eventually of human nature. The second principle which MacIntyre advocates is that virtue ethics concerns itself the way in which the self is to be conceived as a unity. This is required because moral life lived by the self or the moral agent is to be conceived as something more than a disconnected set of piecemeal action or *ad hoc* acts of the will during the course of one's life. MacIntyre also wishes to move away from the modern moral theories back to Aristotle but without a theory of human nature which he calls Aristotle's metaphysical biology. He hopes to recover the common morality of the West with the help of the above mentioned two principles which he discovers as follows. Firstly, for the unity of the self, he looks to the characters in narratives. The unity of the self is like a unity exhibited in a story or a narrative. For MacIntyre, thus, the narratival identity of a moral agent is placed within a much larger and a more pervasive narrative of the society in which he is placed. These narratives give meaning and direction to the virtues which explain why different cultures embody different orders of virtues.

For the second principle mentioned above, that is, for the teleological scheme, also MacIntyre looks up to societal narratives. MacIntyre observes that every culture already has a recognizable hierarchy of virtues reflected in the structures of the community narratives project certain tasks which are considered most valuable for the members of that community and other tasks which are left to individual satisfaction thus set up a hierarchy of virtues appropriate to the hierarchy of task in question. Further, since the unity of the individual self in a given society itself is a part of the unity of the cultural narratives, the individual's *telos* is no other than the goal which his culture specifies as the most valuable object. We have then something like the Aristotelian ethics without his philosophy of nature.

In the modern world, however, MacIntyre faces the problem that the culture narratives of different classes (caste, ethnic and religious groups) are notable to recommend what virtues are to be retained and what are to be discarded for ethical reasons. We find that the major objectives recommended within a society refer to secular goals though often the virtues recommended to attain these goals are drawn from religious quarters. So, there is a problem as to how these virtues are to be made relevant to objectives appropriate to several goals. It would seem that if ethics is to serve as the foundation of social relationship between different social groups, then in the modern world of 'plural' societies, we need some kind of culture-transcended mega narratives for mankind.

Recently, Russell Hittinger has advanced what appears to be the most powerful argument against MacIntyre's approach. Since I am more concerned with the logic of Virtue ethics, I shall ignore the particular internal criticism on MacIntyre by his numerous critics and proceed to discuss Hittinger more seriously. Hittinger argues :

> Granted that virtues, as moral qualities or properties, represent a certain ratio or intelligibility of moral agency, the question naturally arises whether there is an ordinatio, a non-arbitrary principle of order, which would allow us to assess how these virtues ought to fit together.[4]

His answer is that MacIntyre's approach cannot provide the required ordinatio. The point here is that people do not subscribe to mere list of virtues. The list of virtues, as has been observed by many, is lengthy and mostly unordered and also theoretically formless. In other words, taken by themselves, virtues and vices are plural, irreducible and incommensurable, and they involve qualities which in practice carry different weight:

> There is usually a form imposed upon the virtues, and the pattern can differ greatly depending, for instance, upon whether one is a Christian or a Stoic. This, however, implies only that specific lists will always turn out to reflect a concrete way of life, and therefore, any particular conception of the virtues is obviously relative to time and circumstance or to background beliefs about God, nature and human nature.[5]

Hittinger's point is that virtues and vices must be seen in the concrete pattern of a way of life so that we can attach relative weight to them according as we understand God, nature and human nature. Thus, disagreements over the pattern or hierarchy of virtues is equivalent to disagreements over morality as such. Hittinger points out that unless one is prepared to accept a kind of conventionalism, it is absolutely essential to inquire into the principles governing the hierarchical ordinatio of virtues. In other words, Virtue Ethics cannot ignore traditional concerns with issues of truth and falsity pertaining to the nature of the world and the meaning of God and human nature. It is always possible that one or more of the world-views turn out to be superior in terms of truth and thus provide a more significant meaning to our moral beliefs. In other words, we need to know what a human being truly ought to be and in respect of this one kind of belief may be closer to truth than another and therefore, preferable to the other. But MacIntyre is content with societal narratives which he considers sufficient to provide both the ratio and ordinatio of virtues. This, however, is deeply unsatisfactory, especially in the fast changing societies of today, the ordinatio of the virtues is constantly in flux and the ratio of virtues is open to idiosyncratic interpretations.

This problem could be avoided by introducing another type of virtue ethics propounded by Pincoffs which upholds a non-teleological functionalist perspective. To help virtue ethics out of these problems, an interesting suggestion has been made by Pincoffs. In his book *Quandaries and Virtues*, he develops a non-teleological functionalist approach to ethics. He outlines the major concerns of the virtue ethicians as follows :

> . . . the structures known as ethical theories are more threats to moral sanity and balance than instruments for their attainment. They have these malign characteristics principally because they are, by nature reductive. They restrict and warp moral reflection by their insistence that moral

> considerations are related in some hierarchical order.[6]

Pincoffs considers the standard moral theories to be reductive in the sense which we have already explained. He rightly points out that in doing ethics in this way, the standard theories ignore the moral assessment of persons, actions and practices that do not fit into the dominant problematic of these theories. As a result, moral insight and judgment fail to display the rich experience and language of morals which we actually possess. In his own non-teleological functionalism, the perspective suggested is as follows :

> The functionalist perspective is that of an engineer, rather than that of the captain of the ship. Wherever the captain may want to go, the engine and working parts of the ship must operate well if he is to get there. We can say things about the optimum performance of the ship and about it a necessary condition of optimum performance that presuppose nothing about the courses of it is to follow.[7]

In Pincoff's view, virtues are simply the qualities which make for good performance. And the "good" here is not determined by reference to a supervenient common and which the individual is to aim at. There are a number of alternative patterns of moral life available to him from which he is to make his 'large choices'. What moral philosophy is to do is to make the individual moral agent aware of what is involved in choosing this rather than the alternative and by that what other forms of life he will commit himself to. And virtues are simply those qualities which will enable him to choose well in full understanding of the problem and the relative defensibility or indefensibility of whatever he chooses. The moral philosopher can seek to discover :

> . . . the reasons for preferring one moral configuration to another and to present alternative patterns of the moral life, not as alternative modes for the resolution of problems, but in the interest of heightening the student's understanding of the nature and relative defensibility or indefensibility of the large choices that he must make.[8]

In this non-teleological functionalism, Pincoffs suggests that virtues themselves do not need to be ordered according to some higher principle. They are all required for the good performance of the moral agent, like the engine and the working parts of the ship which must operate well if the captain is to get them where he wants to go :

> We can say things about the optimum performance of the ship and about what is necessary condition of optimum performance that presupposes nothing about the courses is to follow.[9]

Now, I am not inclined to accept the functionalist account of virtue, for I do not see how it is going to be meaningful without some account of the nature and the character of "The engine". We can talk of the optimum performance of an engine only if we know what a given engine is supposed to do irrespective of what it is fitted to. But in case of a human being, we cannot dissociate the idea of his "optimum performance" from the ends which "the pilot" may want to pursue. The performance of an engine is an end in itself in this sense. How the engine is used is another matter. But there is no parallel to this in the case of a human engine. Thus, we cannot give content to the notion of 'virtues necessary for optimum performance', independent of a *telos* in view. At the most, we can specify in a general manner, some conditions necessary for any human performance, such as physical fitness, intelligence etc. but that does not throw light on their ethical significance to justify their being called "virtues". Ethical Virtues are valued for their own sake and not just because they are necessary to a high-level performance not because they represent 'capacities' to follow the right set of rules or the ideal.

REFERENCES

1. Alasdair MacIntyre. *After Virtue,* London: Duckworth, 1985, p. 21.
2. *Ibid.,* p. 60.
3. *Ibid.,* p. 156.
4. Russell Hittinger. After MacIntyre: Natural Law Theory, Virtue Ethics, and Eudaimonia. *International Philosophical Quarterly,* Fordhum University, December 1989.
5. Russell Hittinger. *Op. cit.,* p. 452.
6. Edmund L. Pincoffs. *Quandaries and Virtues : Against Reductivism in Ethics.*Lawrence : University Press of Kansas, 1986, p. 3.
7. *Ibid.,* p. 7.
8. *Ibid.,* p. 50.
9. *Ibid.,* p. 7.

7

A CRITIQUE OF VIRTUE ETHICS

We are now in a position to take an overall view of Virtue Ethics and arrive at a judgment on whether or not their approach to moral philosophy can and should replace the Act Morality. First, their attack on Act Morality does seem to have great merit. In particular their claim that moral properties do not pertain only to individual acts but to persons, social practices and, more problematically to the world of interpersonal relationships. This means that Act morality is from the very start, is open to the charge of being a very limited enterprise and therefore, a call to a more comprehensive approach such as we find in Virtue Ethics is required. That is, moral philosophy requires a way of judging and a way of recommending acts which are essentially inseparable from persons whose acts they are and also inseparable from the social context in which they exist. Let us now try to see if Virtue Ethics can prove wholly satisfactory in this regard. The biggest problem with Virtue Ethics seems to arise when we consider the fact that the different religions or cultures seem to provide different list of virtues and there can be considerable disagreement over the pattern or hierarchy of the virtues. This amounts to real disagreement over morality as such. This point is made very well by Russell Hittinger who writes :

> Thus, unless one is prepared to rest in a kind of conventionalism, and inquiry into the principles governing hierarchical ordinatio of the Virtues is absolutely critical. A return to Virtue Ethics cannot

> be an excuse for receding from the traditional concern with issues of truth and falsity. By truth and falsity here is meant the status of those claims that Pincoffs says pertain to the nature and meaning of God, the world, and human nature. Nor should one rule out, in advance, the possibility that one or more of these is superior in terms of truth and that, on this basis itself, one may fundamentally reconsider what is of moral concern. Indeed, if no universal principles can be found, it not only means that rival patterns of the moral life are fundamentally irresolvable, but also suggests that nearly all of the significant versions of pre-modern virtue ethics were essentially mistaken about themselves. For Aristotelian, Stoic, Christian and Islamic patterns all purported not merely to be in some minimal conformity to nature or in some general way to include virtues but to embody and exemplify what a human being truly ought to be.[1]

So, if ethics is to serve, as it is deemed to, as the foundation of social relationship in different areas of life, then in the modern world of plural society, it has to have some kind of culture-transcendent element. In India today, we are moving fast towards a highly differentiated society on capitalistic line such that the ideal and narratives of different castes and tribes seem to have lost their meanings. With constant growth of scientific education and industrialization more and more social institutions (community loyalty, extended family, marriage, sex, etc.) are breaking down. There is a rise of individualism and structural atomism. In such a state of affairs, it is impossible to identify and give meanings to the contents of virtues.

In general, if ethics is to work, there must be available some way of criticizing the conventional virtues. This is what generally not provided by virtue ethicians, as we have clearly seen in case of MacIntyre. In ethics there must be some way of making self-criticism too. Not everything can be left to individual's choice or to conventions. It is the non-availability of such a critical tool that inevitably leads to what Popper has called "the closed society". The critical tool has to be impersonal and in some sense objective. But I do not mean to say that it has to be found 'outside' a culture. I think *any* culture if it looks hard enough within its axiological resources, will discover its objective foundation. For this, one might look at its 'inner logic', as it were which, as we have seen, always refers to universals. For example, as M.M. Agrawal has argued it can be demonstrated that the recognition of the value of human life is a necessary feature in the human situation. This comes about when we consider the fact that in the ideal form of interpersonal relationship in communal activity, people cooperate with each other for common ends with an understanding of the point or purpose of their pursuits. And in this process, they clearly *assert* the characteristic human attitude towards each other, viz. the attitude of treating each other with the natural presupposition of the unconditional worth or value of human life. That is, to paraphrase an epithet of Wittgenstein's as done by Agrawal :

> My attitude towards human life is an attitude towards what is to ultimate worth. I am not of the opinion that human life has value.[2]

There is no doubt that there are such universal human values presupposed by the value-systems of every culture. But their utility as the required critical tool is very limited. It is limited by the fact that the universal values, having no empirical content of their own are open to various interpretations, and in actual life, they are cashed in many different norms of behaviour. For example, the Mongolian Chuckchi tribesman who puts to death his old and infirm grandfather by a severe blow on his head is guided by the same value of life as the young African who starves himself to keep his elder alive till the latter's natural death. In actual life, the universal values turn culture-specific. So, we have to look for the impersonal and objective character of ethics in something else. Virtue ethicians have not been able to reach out to the universals from the culture-specifics in ethics.

Before presenting my own reflections on this matter, however, we must consider briefly what P.F. Strawson suggests in his essay 'Social Morality and Individual Ideal' (included in his *Freedom and Consent*). For, Strawson's position is an excellent example of an effort to reconcile the opposing demands of universality and pluralism in ethics. Strawson concedes that there is a nexus of universality in all moralities. First, there is the formal requirement of the 'abstract virtue of justice' which demands that :

> A man should not insist on a particular claim while refusing to acknowledge any reciprocal claim. But from this purely formal feature of morality, we cannot justify the *application* of an actually accepted moral rule for a particular situation or society.[3]

Fortunately, apart from this formal requirement there are other more concrete features of morality which are universal :

> It is also important to recognize that certain human interests are so fundamental and so general that they must be universally acknowledged in some form and to some degree in any conceivable moral community . . . . the recognition of certain general virtues and obligations will be a logically or humanly necessary feature of almost any conceivable moral system.[4]

These universals and obligations, however, are limited to what he calls the "sphere of morality" which is characterized by these rules which are necessary for the sustenance of the society. Further, he sees the sphere of morality (including, for example, such virtues as honesty and avoidance of injury to others) as a necessary prerequisite to the realization of any human ideal at all. Morality is then distinguished from the "sphere of the ethical" which is much larger than the former. But, unfortunately, in this region, relativism reigns supreme :

> Men make for themselves pictures of ideal forms of life. Such pictures are various, and may be sharp opposition to each other; and one and the same individual may be captivated by different and sharply conflicting pictures at different times.[5]

Further, these pictures are not conjured up out of the blue as it were. Behind these pictures, lie certain 'profound truths' about life and the world. These profound truths capture the 'ethical imagination' of man and lead him to produce 'pictures of ideal forms of life' some examples from his list of such pictures would show how diverse they can be : the ideal of self-obliterating devotion to duty or to the service of others; of asceticism, contemplation and retreat; of action, dominance and power, of the cultivation of an exquisite sense of the luxurious; etc.

These ideals portray whole ways of life; they tell us how to conduct the affairs of our life. But despite diversity, there is no need of despair. Strawson thinks that an enlightened ethical consciousness will recognize the validity of the 'universal general virtues and obligations' and at the same time, it will be 'in sympathy with a variety of conflicting ideals of life'. Such a man will make no attempt to resolve the conflict. Rather, he would admire the evaluative diversity of his society and choose to live according to his own ideals as and when he gets captivated by one or the other.

It is clear that Strawson's rather romantic vision of a truly human society is too unrealistic. It seems to leave everything as it is. At most, any 'picture' is valid as an ideal, except, perhaps, an ideal of trying to impose one's ideal upon others.

Of course, they are based on 'profound truths' about life and the world. But the truths are many and they are incommensurate. Their profundity depends simply upon the impression of the subject. In case of a clash, there is no objective way of settling which truth is more valuable than the other, or for that matter, if it is a truth at all. And 'sympathy' or admiration of diversity' do not seem to be helpful here. Similarly, one is supposed to leave the conflict of ideals unresolved. But in actual life, one simply cannot, short of total withdrawal from society, take this position. The pursuit of conflicting individual ideals is the major cause of actual social conflict resulting in violence and all its accompanying social ills. And surely if ethics has any social purpose, it is the resolution of conflict. Whatever ideal one may choose to live by, it remains central to ethics to inform us that we relate to others in such a way as to reduce conflict to the minimum. An ethically matured society must be conflict-free society. Ethics is the total *order* in life.

However, from what we have said so far, it is clear that such ethics cannot be found in the *systems* of virtues, values or ideals, or in ideology, all of which land us in conflict. In modern societies which are in a state of constant change, the individual has greater personal freedom to choose. But in the face of a daunting pluralism of values, and the absence of any objective basis for preference, how is one to choose? If one simple succumbs to the will of one's conditioned past, and adopts the virtues and the *telos* of the cultural stream, one happens to be flowing in; one becomes a victim of conventionalism. One cannot leave one's 'ethical imagination' to chance, to capture whatever comes by it. Ethics must make us capable of choosing meaningfully.

With recent discoveries in ecological and environmental studies, science has made us aware that if we are to survive, there has to be a spirit of cooperation with the universe as a whole with other living beings and the things of nature. But man has completely lost the spirit of cooperation. In its place, what we see is domination, manipulation and destruction.

Why does man live like this? The answer is to be found in his 'spiritual' condition. He is disillusioned, isolated and fragmented. And sadly our laws, our governments, our religions, all emphasize the separateness of man bringing about more fragmentation. As Krishnamurthy observes :

> One can see in all social structures the destructive effect of fragmentation taking place — nation against nation, one group against another group, one family against another family, one individual against another. It is the same religiously, socially and economically. Each one is striving for himself, for his class or his particular interest in the community. This division of beliefs, ideals, conclusions and prejudices is preventing the spirit of cooperation from flowing. We are human beings, not tribal identities, exclusive, separate, we are human beings caught in conclusions, theories, faiths. It is our human circumstances that make us search for food, clothes and shelter at the expense of others. Our very thinking is separative and all action springing from this limited thought must prevent cooperation. The economic and social structure, as it is now, including organized religions, intensifies exclusiveness, separateness. This lack of cooperation ultimately brings about wars and the destruction of man. It is only during crises or disasters that we seem to come together, and when they are over, we are back to our old condition. We seem to be incapable of living and working together harmoniously.[6]

So the task of ethics is to show us the way of living and working together harmoniously. But as we have seen, this way is to be found in 'the way of the ideal' or 'the way of the system'. There is no 'recipe book' for good life. So the ethical question, "How is one to live?" Is not a question, about what or how one is to *choose,* but is a question about what kind of person one is to be so that one is capable of living and working harmoniously with others. This point has been grasped well by the virtue ethicians. But as we have seen, the general answer that 'one should live by a scheme of virtues' does not take us far enough.

There are other practical problems concerning the cultivation and practice of virtues and even concerning the existential status of virtues. Prof. M.M. Agrawal argues :

> The post-modern reaction to modern ethical theories seems to be along the right lines. As we have seen, it recommends that moral thinkers should turn their attention away from problematics to the person as a whole and to the ancient ideal of the 'good man' — the good man when Aristotle described as the very embodiment of practical reason. But who or what is a good man, the ideal ethical agent? We have seen that thinking of the good man in terms of the possessor of virtues faces the initial problem arising out of the fact that there are several different lists of virtues in the offing and virtues are incommensurate. But there are other more serious problems with 'virtues'. Strictly speaking, it seems to me, that virtues can neither be cultivated nor practiced. How, for example, as an adult, one is to self-consciously, make oneself courageous? To begin to cultivate courage one will have to go back to the beginning and sow the seeds of it in oneself in one's childhood. Moreover, the seeds have to be sown on the right 'soil' and allowed to grow in the right environment. These cannot be created at all, least of all recreated by conscious effort in one's own case. Nor can the virtues be practiced in the sense that one can self-consciously decide to act courageously. And more importantly, even if one has grown to be courageous one cannot make an ethical use of it unless his courage is well-integrated with his

> passions and emotions within the right view of human life. For, as Kant has said, that courage in the breast of a scoundrel makes him even more abominable.[7]

I agree with the above mentioned comments in the sense that in actual life it is indeed difficult to dissociate the growth of virtues in a person from his chance-situation in the society concerning his upbringing and the occasions for the use of his personal freedom. It is difficult to determine who is truly a virtuous man : One who is moved by compassion or the one who is moved by the sense of duty? We can even imagine a virtuous man who is in a certain situation torn between the demands of compassion and sense of duty. Such a virtuous person may eventually end up by doing nothing or for that matter by committing suicide. Virtue ethicians seem to picture a virtuous man as a man unaffected by sudden emotion and the persuasion of desire. This is, to say the least, an unrealistic picture.

REFERENCES

1. *Op. cit.*, p. 453.
2. M. M. Agrawal. Morals and the Value of Human Life, *Journals of Indian Council of Philosophical Research*, 111/2, 1986.
3. P. F. Strawson. *Essay on Social Morality and Individual Ideal.*
4. Christian Ethics and Contemporary Philosophy, Edited by T. T. Ramsay, S. C. M., 1966, p. 291.
5. *Op. cit.*, p.280.
6. *Ibid., Krishnamurti : Letters to the Schools*, Krishnamurti Foundation India. Madras, 1986, p. 87.
7. M.M. Agrawal. *Ethics and Spirituality.* Indian Institute of Advanced Study, Rashtrapati Nivas, Simla, 1998, p. 12.

8

CONCLUSION

In the concluding chapter I wish to take stock of what I have said in the earlier chapters, and to draw some general conclusions with respect to the problems that I have addressed to myself in the thesis. The focus of the problem, it will be recalled, is the recent controversy between what I have called Act Morality and the development subsumed under the title Virtue Ethics.

Traditionally, in moral philosophy there have been two sets of concepts competing with each other for precedence. On the one hand, there are teleological concepts introduced most judiciously by Aristotle such as *Eudaimonia* or happiness or well-being or in more popular modern utilitarian literature, the desirable and pleasurable or the good. These concepts have to do with the ultimate and proper goals or ends of human life towards which moral actions should be directed. On the other hand, there are the deontological concepts which have to do with duties, with rights and wrong conducts and with moral responsibility for one's action. In general, the teleological *ethicians* hold that deontological concepts are secondary and subsidiary to their own concepts. In other words, they maintain that no behaviour can be considered morally right or praiseworthy unless it is conducive to realization of the ultimate good or has desirable consequences. The moral justification of a given act or a piece of behaviour must, in the end, be related to its capacity to promote good or human well-being. In contrast with this, the deontologist holds that duty, rightness and moral responsibility are independent of teleological concepts. This independence is logical. That is, an act is morally right and it could be one's duty to perform it even if we were not clear or did not know the nature of its consequences. Of course, most of the acts which the deontologist recommends to us, do in actuality tend to promote human happiness, but this fact is not treated as the ground for judging them morally right or wrong.

In other words, for the teleologist, an act is right if and only if it is conducive to human happiness because the very meaning of "right" is that it is conducive to man. On the other hand, for deontologist, the rightness of conduct has nothing to do with its conduciveness to man. These two concepts have completely different meanings.

The teleological principles have been held by Aristotle, Epicurus, St. Thomas and in modern times by the utilitarians such as Bentham and John S. Mill and even more recently reinvoked by Alasdair MacIntyre in the form of what has come to be known as Virtue Ethics. Almost all the great classical philosophers have at least implicitly made a reference to the teleological principle. On the other hand, the most famous of the deontologists Immanuel Kant would be much less popular today since general tendency of the contemporary man is again not to hold moral principles in their absolute form. For Kant, as we have seen, it would have been morally wrong to tell a lie even to save an innocent man's life, which would hardly be acceptable to us today. On the other hand, even the teleological principles could not be upheld at any cost, as it were. As for example, if God were to offer salvation to a whole race of people in return for one of their children to be tormented eternally in hell, it will be considered morally unacceptable.

The problematic in my thesis, however, cuts across the teleological-deontological distinction. In modern moral theories, we find something common to both types of theories. This common element is the fact that modern moral theories consider individual acts of individual people as the primary object of moral evaluation. Thus, the utilitarian teleologists and Kantian deontologists both attempt to devise schemes in order to determine whether individual acts are right or wrong. This is not surprising to consider the rise of individualism and the role of law so characteristic of the modern society. As we have noted earlier, modern moral philosophy, at least, since the time of Thomas Hobbes, has been concerned with discovering a fundamental moral principle from which rules, supposed to govern individual acts could be arrived at. In modern moral philosophy, therefore, it has been a major pre-occupation of philosophers to find *rational justification* for their fundamental principles as well as for the procedure to judge the rightness or wrongness of individual acts. In this endeavour, various theories on both sides have been put forward. But none has stood the test of time. Indeed, as MacIntyre has pointed out, moral discourse in our time has reached several dead ends and absurd moral theories such as various versions of Emotivism have been put forward.

It is with appearance of MacIntyre's writing especially his *After Virtue* that moral philosophy seems to have taken a new turn away from the modernists such as utilitarians, Kantians and more recently the emotivists. In the wake of MacIntyre's writing several moral philosophers have reached against the modern theories which I have called Act Morality. It has produced a good deal of literature on moral philosophy which is considered under the title of Virtue Ethics. The virtue ethicians, however, are not teleologists. I have discussed one major theory of Edmund Pincoffs, who is a non-teleological functionalist virtue ethician. In general, however, virtue ethicians discredit Act Morality on various counts and pronounce it dead. In their view, moral philosophy should turn its attention away from problematics to persons and from "decisional procedures" to the study of human character and virtue. In this way, the virtue ethicians claim to replace Act Morality with Virtue Ethics. Are they likely to succeed in this effort? The debate is still going on but my thesis is an attempt to answer this question considered in its various ramifications.

Before proceeding further, however, it will be useful to make the following distinction which applied to both types of theories mentioned above. The first distinction is between the ways in which the rightness of an action may be looked upon. One is when an action is considered right *objectively or subjectively.* We can explain this by an example from its use by utilitarians. As we have noted, according to utilitarianism, the ultimate good which is to be aimed at, is captured by the formula "the greatest happiness of the greatest number". Thus, if an act of a particular kind, for example, promise-keeping is to be declared objectively right then it does in fact promote the greatest good of the greatest number. But it is clear that a moral agent could be mistaken in his personal belief about what promotes the greatest happiness, and therefore, also in his belief about what he ought to do. It is also clear that an act leading to the greatest happiness of the greatest number, may be performed not only from morally desirable motive but also from morally neutral or even morally undesirable motive. For example, a mother might leave her child on the footpath just because she cannot look after it hoping that some Mother Teresa would pick it up and that would promote the best interest of all. Nevertheless, the mother's act will not be considered as morally commendable. Further, many acts which would lead to the greatest happiness if performed, cannot be performed simply because of the limits of human freedom. Thus to say that an act is *subjectively* right is to say that the agent believes the act to be right, that the act is performed from morally acceptable motive and that the agent is free to perform it. This definition of 'subjective right' can be applied without its modification to non-utilitarian as well as to utilitarian theories. The definition of objective right given above, however, varies from one situation to another depending upon the criterion of right conduct employed.

The second distinction which will be helpful is that which exists between a particular act or course of behaviour and the general type or kind of behaviour. This distinction is particularly helpful in understanding the deontological ethics and plays a role even in utilitarian and other teleological theories. In these latter theories, the formal definition of 'objectively right' is the same whether it be a question of a particular act or a class of acts, whether we are evaluating the concrete behaviour of a given individual in a given situation or a general moral rule relating to a kind of behaviour that might be performed by anyone. A particular act is justified by demonstrating that it is conducive to the well-being of man and a moral rule pertaining to a certain kind of behaviour is justified in the same way. Since, however, a given concrete act may be an instance of several kinds of behaviour conforming perhaps to one moral rule while violating another, it does not follow that an act is objectively right simply because it conforms to a given moral rule. Thus, teleologists generally tend to consider moral rule only as rules of thumb. In general, it is held that we must tell the truth because, telling the truth is good. It is also held to do what is necessary, for example, the only way to save a man's life is to tell a lie, therefore, one is obliged to tell a lie. It must not be thought, however, that the teleologist demands that every choice be preceded by lengthy deliberation. Moral rules may only be rules of thumb, but most of them reflect the collective wisdom of past human experience, and unless they came into conflict, most teleologists would regard the very fact of their existence as a sufficiently good reason on the basis of the following.

Now with this distinction in mind, we can proceed to consider some detailed criticisms of the two types of theories with the focus on the distinction between what we have called Act Morality and Virtue Ethics. In chapters 2 and 3, I have considered two representative types of theories, namely utilitarianism and Kantianism. Although from what has been said above, it appears that the utilitarians are teleologists while Kant is the most ideal deontologist, in my considerations, both could come under the title of Act Morality which as we have seen, focuses upon the evaluation of particular acts providing their own kind of fundamental principle together with a philosophical justification for it. In evaluating Act Morality my strategy is first of all to make a broad distinction between "internal' and "external" argument against the theories concerned. The internal argument is roughly meant to focus upon the internal consistency and coherence of their proposal. The external argument, on the other hand, is meant to evaluate the motive, the scope and the methods of these theories with respect to their claims for being the only right type of theory in moral philosophy. Similar approach is followed in case of the evaluation of Virtue Ethics.

One major type of Act Morality which I have considered in my thesis is utilitarianism. In this, the good which human action needs to realize is happiness. The criterion of right action is that the consequences of any action should lead to the greatest happiness of the greatest number of people in the given situation. The basic internal argument against this approach concerns the calculation of the consequences envisaged. Bentham has suggested that happiness should be calculated in terms of pleasure produced by an action counting the number of people affected by it. The problem is that the calculation of pleasures is most illusive. Firstly, the word 'pleasure' does not seem to connote one property or quality common to all the pleasure-giving acts. Each pleasure-giving act seems to have its own kind of pleasure. The pleasure of playing cricket or watching it played is not the same as sexual pleasure, for example. Moreover, the same type of pleasure may not be derived from the same act by everyone. Furthermore, pleasure derived from a given act varies both in quantity and in intensity from individual to individual. All the factors governing the amount of pleasure make it almost impossible to calculate the amount of happiness which will accrue upon the individual concerned. Late J.S. Mill added the qualitative dimension to the calculation of happiness. He claims that some pleasures are intrinsically 'better' than others raising the question whether the higher pleasures produced for fewer members will be preferable to the production of lower pleasure for larger numbers. This is well summed up in his well known dictum:

> "It is better to be a Socrates dissatisfied than a pig satisfied."

The effect of noticing the complexity of the calculation led Sidgwick almost to a point of breakdown. He exclaimed :

> "Where I expected the cosmos I found only chaos". Sidgwick's realization resulted in a severe modification of the existing utilitarian position. He maintains that it is not only pleasures but several other things (for example, knowledge, love, etc.), or good, and human action will be right in aiming at any of these things. What the things are is known by rational intuition. The net result of Sidgwick's realization was to introduce a great deal of subjectivity into determination of what is good. It is especially difficult to determine the order of preference of these intuited values.

The other representative theory of Act Morality which I have considered is the deontological theory of Kant. Kant provided the supreme principle of morality called the categorical imperative in three of its formulations. The first concerns the *form* on the categorical imperative; the second concerns its content; and the third links these two together. These are as follows :

1. Act as if you were legislating for everyone.

2. Act so as to treat human beings always as end and never merely as means.
3. Act as if you were a member of a realm of ends.

Kant thought that all these formulations are equivalent and represent the same essence of morality. But as we have seen, they are not quite equivalent as they project different meanings and apply to different aspects of a given action. Even then, the main internal objection to Kant's thesis concerns the question of its application to real life situation. It is observed by the critics that its application cannot be successful without importing through the back door, the very naturalism which Kant is so eager to avoid. For example, in considering the second formulation stated above, we can raise the question "What does it mean to treat people as ends in themselves?" In one interpretation, which is a utilitarian interpretation; if you treat every person as an end, you show regard to their desire and you must, as and when you can, help them to fulfil their desires. Since it is generally believed that everyone desires happiness for oneself and freedom from pain and suffering, to treat all human beings as ends would mean that one should act for the promotion of their happiness and prevention of unhappiness. But this amounts to saying that happiness is the supreme moral good. But this is far from Kant's original intention in formulating the categorical imperative. Since, as we have seen, Kant announces right in the beginning that the only thing which is unconditionally good is the good will which manifests itself in acting for the sake of duty and it is to find this out, that is, to find out if the motive for duty as the sole motive is present in the proposed action, that Kant advocates the

> categorical imperative. In other words, the application of any of the formulations of the categorical imperative is supposed to show if the proposed action were the embodiment of good will and not whether it would be conducive to production of the natural property of happiness. Similar considerations apply to cases of other formulations of the categorical imperative.

We can now move to consider the external objection to Act Morality which applies to both, the utilitarian and the Kantian, that is, to the teleological as well as the deontological versions of it. My discussion on these versions in the earlier chapters are relevant to our tasks of determining the relative merit of Act Morality *vis-à-vis* Virtue Ethics.

The first major charge against Act Morality is that modern moral theories are "reductive". By this is meant that all consideration of rights and wrong, good and bad are reduced to a single paradigm represented in the fundamental principle of moral evaluation represented in the concerned theory. For example, as we noted in the case of utilitarianism all cases of moral rightness are to be determined by the sole criterion of consideration of the consequences of the proposed action. Similarly, in the deontological theory, that is, the Kantian theory, as for example, all considerations have to be reduced to the consideration of whether or not the maxim of any proposed action is "universalizable". The objection to this procedure is that it is too simplistic and ignores the extraordinary richness and variety of moral considerations relevant to the determination of the moral quality of an action. The second main external objection concerns the scope of application of modern moral theories. A point which virtue ethicians emphasize is that traditionally ethics has been concerned primarily not with evaluation of individual acts but with evaluation of persons and their lives considered as a "whole". In this context, moral terms are directly applied to the qualities of character of persons; judging of action as right and wrong is secondary and it is performed by judging whether the act is of a kind which a virtuous man would typically perform it or not. In other words, Act Morality tends to limit the scope of moral philosophy by turning away from persons and their character to the consideration of individual acts only. Both these types of objections seem to me quite valid. Finally, another serious objection comes from the fact that Act Morality is unable to explain the acts of supererogation and acts coming under what Bernard Williams has called "thick" moral notions. Supererogatory acts are neither duties nor acts which are nearly right. Thus, they cannot be subjected to assessment by the application of either the utilitarian or the Kantian supreme moral principle of morality. But do they destroy the credibility of Act Morality altogether? And if they do, could the approach of Virtue Ethics restore the credibility of moral philosophy? These are the questions I proceed to answer in the remaining part of this chapter.

In answer to the first question I have already suggested in my evaluation of Act Morality that when we look at the real life situation of moral evaluation, we often come across cases where the application of one or other type of Act Morality clearly has a sway. A certain action may, for example, be clearly wrong due to overwhelmingly bad consequences even though it may be in some sense considered as a duty or indeed an act which is expected of a virtuous person. For example, 'Socrates' drinking the hemlock while he had the option to escape is clearly wrong on utilitarian ground. If he had lived, he would have been a revolutionary force bringing a lot of good to correct society at that time. But by drinking the hemlock virtuously he had avoided the moral responsibility which is placed upon any citizen of his status. The point that I am making is that in real life situation, we often have to quite deliberately set about to make a choice in the light of an objective principle rather than our vague personal intuitions. The availability of such principle, therefore, can be an asset rather than a problem for the individual moral agent. The fact that such principle does not apply to all and sundry does not seem to be important. Moreover, in the corporate world of today one has often to make moral judgment independent of personal virtues and intentions. In such situation, one can only lean upon the generally recognized moral principle available to him. Act Morality, thus, has a place in our day-to-day moral life. On the other hand, if we take a concrete example of a corporate activity as a whole, we may find that a serious ethical problem arises right in the beginning. Consider the case of cigarette manufacturers. It is common knowledge backed by scientific research that cigarette smoking is extremely harmful not only to the smokers but to the non-smokers sitting around them. The company seems to exonerate itself by putting a warning on cigarette packet to the effect that smoking is injurious to health. But if we go right to the beginning and ask if a Company should undertake such an enterprise at all, then the answer could be different. It seems to me that a virtuous individual entrepreneur will not undertake to introduce in the social life of the community something which is so indisputable harmful as cigarette. Such considerations and others, as we have seen, give leverage to Virtue Ethics' point of view.

Let us now look at the case of Virtue Ethics, if it can offer a better alternative to Act Morality. In the earlier chapters, I have discussed two types of Virtue Ethics with special reference to those of MacIntyre and Pincoffs. This is because MacIntyre's is a brand of teleological ethics somewhat akin to Aristotle, while Pincoffs's theory is a version of non-teleological Virtue Ethics. There are a number of objections to both these types of theories which are internal and specific to these theories.

However, as in the case of Act Morality, here too, what I have called the external arguments, are more important for my thesis. In this respect, the most outstanding dissatisfaction with Virtue Ethics comes from the fact that virtue ethicians are unable to supply either the *ratio* or the *ordinatio* of virtues. By 'ratio' I have this in mind : Virtues are supposed to be the qualities of character which can activate the moral agent to produce the right kind of behaviour even in the most complicated kind of moral situation. But virtues are not merely instrumental in producing the required objective they are supposed to be at once both good in themselves as well as instrumentally good. But what makes a certain quality of character good in this sense? No satisfactory answer is to be found in MacIntyre, while in Pincoffs, the goodness of virtues is solely considered in the light of their efficiency in reaching out to the supposed goal. But then one would have thought that the goals themselves would be shown to be morally desirable. Pincoffs does not do this; instead, he leaves it to the individual to choose for himself in the light of the pros and cons of choosing one of the alternatives. This procedure, however, does not show why the virtues invoked should be considered intrinsically good as it is required by any serious virtue ethics.

The idea of ordinatio is as follows : Virtues, it will be agreed, are not simply amorphous values both the meaning and direction of virtues are obtained from the narratives in which they have a place. The Christian virtues, for example, can be understood only in relation to the Biblical narratives where man is seen as *homo viator*, that is, a pilgrim. In other words, virtues derive their meaning by being embodied in concrete patterns of life. Reference to such narratives serve as the criterion or the ordinatio of virtues. It tells us not only their meaning but also how to *order* the virtues into a coherent scheme. Such an ordering is required by practical ethics, especially in situations of conflict. A virtuous man may also be pulled on occasions in different directions of opposite temptations. He will then have to consult, what may be called his inner table of virtues in an ordered fashion.

Moreover, the narratives are the embodiments of truths about man, the world and God. Such pictures of truth are impersonal and provide justification for ordering the virtues within concrete pattern of lives. But such truths are many. For example, the Christian, the Buddhist, the Islamic patterns of lives are sufficiently different from each other and even offer many points of opposition to the other. It may be possible to determine the superiority of one pattern over the other. But to do this, we would need a mega narrative. In the absence of such a narrative, it is not possible to choose between different narratives, religious or otherwise, available to man, and consequently it is not possible to order the virtues which a moral agent may invoke in actual life.

Furthermore, there seems to be some ambiguity in the notion of thc 'virtuous man' itself. When we ask the question who is a virtuous man, we tend to get different answers. Is the virtuous man, for example, the man who is overwhelmingly moved by love and compassion, or the one who is moved by the sense of duty alone. Or is he the one who is constantly aware of the conflict within himself and, therefore, ends up by doing whatever seems to him right at the moment or perhaps being torn between the pursuit of conflicting ends becomes a cynic? It is hard to give a clear answer to this question. Recently, Act Moralists have argued that virtue is nothing but a single strong *disposition* to act according to a supreme moral principle or if one is a deontologist, to act from the absolute principle of doing one's duty for the sake of duty. But this dispositional account of virtue is totally rejected by the virtue ethicians because it minimizes the value of virtue in ethical conduct. Virtues must be considered as qualities of character in such a way that it is conducive to producing a conflict-free activity in constantly new situations facing the individual. Virtue ethicians seem to picture a virtuous man as a man unaffected, on the one hand, by sudden emotions and persuasion of desire, and on the other, fully sensitive to the aesthetic and affective aspects of life. Such a combination of qualities of character governed by a rational principle of wisdom must be rare in an individual. Such considerations make Virtue Ethics looks like the privilege of the few highly educated, or as Bernard Williams says of the "lucky". This obviously limits the scope of Virtue Ethics.

The theories which I have discussed fail to provide the ordinatio of virtues. Nevertheless, they have a point which is that the complexity and the variety of moral life cannot be summed up under a principle such as the theories of Act Morality provides. In this way, they make a rightful place for virtue ethics. In my view, therefore, neither Act Morality nor Virtue Ethics can provide an inclusive moral theory. But both seem to have relevance to our moral lives. And there is no cause for despair in the totalities of moral life which is very rich and complex. Do not give way to a particular theory in understanding it. May be in the end it all comes back to the individual who chooses and how he lives without any ultimate justification for any moral standard. Perhaps, Shakespeare is right :

> Life is a tale
> Told by an idiot
> . . . .
> Full of noise and fury
> Signifying nothing.

BIBLIOGRAPHY

Abelson, Raziel & Marie-Louse Friqueguon (Eds). *Ethics for Modern Life.* Edited by St. Martin's Press, New York, 1991.

Agrawal, M. M. *Consciousness and the Integrated Being. Sartre and Krishnamurti.* IIAS, Shimla, National Publishing House, New Delhi, 1991.

Arrington, Robert L. *Western Ethics: An Historical Introduction,* Blackwell Publishers Inc., 1998.

Churchland, Paul. "The Logical Character of Action Explanations", *Philosophical Review,* 79, 1971.

Danagah, Alan. *Theory of Morality.* Chicago University Press, 1977.

Donagan, Alan. "Consistency in Nationalist Moral System", *Journal of Philosophy,* 81, 1984.

Foot, Phillipa (Eds). *Theories of Ethics.* Oxford University Press, 1967.

Frankena, William. *Ethics.* H. J. Prentice Hall, 1973.

Hare, R.M. *Freedom and Reason.* London : Oxford University Press, 1965.

Hare, R.M. *The Language of Morals.* London : Oxford University Press, 1982.

Harrison, Jonathan. *Our Knowledge of Right and Wrong.* London, George Allen & Unwin Ltd., New York, Humanities Press Inc., 1971.

Hill, Thomas E. "Kant on Imperfect Duty and Supererogation", *Kant Studies,* 62, 1971.

Hittinger, Russell. *The New Natural Law Theory.*

Hollis, Martin and Steven Lukes (Eds.) *Rationality and Relativism,* Oxford Blackwell, 1993.

Hudson, Stephen D. *Human Character and Morality, Reflections from the History of Ideas.* Routledge & Kegan Paul, Boston, London & Henley, 1986.

Hudson, Stephen. "Taking Virtues Seriously", *Australasian Journal of Philosophy,* 59, 1981.

Hudson, W.D. *Ethicial Intuitionism.* London: Macmillan & Company Limited, 1967.

Lawback (Tr.). *Foundations of the Metaphysics of Morals.* Indianapolis, Bobbs-Herrill, 1989.

Lawrence, Blum. *Friendship, Altruism and Morality.* London : Routledge, 1980.

Liddel, Brendan E. A. (Translator), *Kant on the Foundation of Morality,* Indiana University Press, 1970.

Maclntyre, Alasdair. *After Virtue.* Indiana : University of Notre Dame Press, 1981.

Mao, Xavier P. "Hegel on Kant and Morality: An Essay" submitted to the University of Sydney, 1996, p.10. Unpublished.

Murdoch, Irish. *The Sovereignty of Good.* New York-Schockon, 1971.

O'Connor, D. J. *Aquinas and Natural Law.* London : Macmillan & Co. Ltd., 1967.

Pincoffs, Edmund. *Quandaries and Virtues.* Kansas University Press, 1906.

Raphael, D. D. *Moral Philosophy.* Oxford University Press, Oxford, New York, 1994.

Sullivan, Roger J. *Immanuel Kant's Moral Theory.* Cambridge University Press, Cambridge, New York, Por Chester, Melbourne, Sydney, 1991.

Warnock, Mary. *Ethics Since 1900.* Oxford University Press, Amen House, London E.C.4, 1960.

Williams, Bernard. *Moral Luck.* Cambridge : Cambridge University Press, 1985.

Williams, Bernard. *Ethics and the Limits of Philosophy.* Cambridge University Press, 1986.

INDEX